Guidance and Careers

BARRON'S TEEN-AGE SUMMER
GUIDE Reinhold $2.25 paper
SO YOU'RE GOING TO BE A
TEACHER Filbin & Vogel $1.25 paper

College Reviews and Texts

Comprehensive, expertly written literary history and criticism, as well as other subjects to enrich class work, provide material for discussion, papers, and review.

AMERICAN HISTORY
Klose (In 2 volumes)   each $1.95 paper
AMERICAN LITERATURE
Abel (In 3 volumes)   each $2.25 paper
AMERICAN LITERATURE, RECENT
Heiney $2.25 paper
BASIC TOOLS OF RESEARCH
Vitale $1.95 paper
BUSINESS LAW Howard $1.95 paper
CANTERBURY TALES, STUDENTS'
GUIDE TO MacLaine $1.95 paper
CLASSICAL DRAMA, GREEK AND
ROMAN Reinhold $1.95 paper
CLASSICS, GREEK AND ROMAN
Reinhold $1.95 paper
COLLEGE ALGEBRA
Peters $2.25 paper
COMPARATIVE GOVERNMENT
Johnson $1.95 paper
CONTEMPORARY LITERATURE
Heiney $2.25 paper
ENGLISH LITERATURE
Grebanier (2 Vols.)   ea. $1.95 paper
ENGLISH ROMANTIC WRITERS
Battenhouse $1.95 paper
ESSENTIALS OF EFFECTIVE
WRITING Hopper & Gale $1.50 paper
PRACTICE FOR EFFECTIVE
WRITING Hopper & Gale $1.50 paper
WORLD LITERATURE
Hopper & Grebanier
        Vol. 1, $1.50; Vol. 2, $1.75 paper
HISTORY AT A GLANCE
Helmreich   95¢ paper
HISTORY OF EDUCATION
Frost $1.25 paper
PRINCIPLES OF GEOGRAPHY
Guernsey, Doerr & Van Cleef $1.95 paper
PRINCIPLES OF PHYSICAL
GEOGRAPHY
Guernsey, Doerr & Van Cleef $1.95 paper
READING SHAKESPEARE'S PLAYS:
A Guide for College Students
Price $1.25 paper
SHAKESPEARE COMEDIES, TRAG-
EDIES, HISTORIES, HIGHLIGHTS OF
Vandiver $1.95 paper
SPELLING YOUR WAY TO SUCCESS
Mersand   98¢ paper

College Preparation

Tops with guidance counselors all over the country.

HOW TO PREPARE FOR COLLEGE
ENTRANCE EXAMINATIONS
Brownstein & Weiner $2.50 paper
BARRON'S GUIDE TO THE
TWO-YEAR COLLEGES
Eskow $2.98 paper
COLLEGE BOUND (Third Revised
Edition) Brownstein $1.98 paper
YOU CAN WIN A SCHOLARSHIP
Brownstein $3.95 paper
HOW TO PREPARE FOR COLLEGE
BOARD ACHIEVEMENT TESTS:
   ENGLISH Shostak $1.75 paper
   FRENCH Cabat & Godin $1.50 paper
   GERMAN Newmark & S. $2.25 paper
   LATIN Gerwig $2.25 paper
   SPANISH Cabat & Godin $1.75 paper
   BIOLOGY Bleifeld $2.25 paper
   CHEMISTRY Snyder $2.25 paper
   PHYSICS Gewirtz $2.25 paper
   SOCIAL STUD. Midgley $1.75 paper
MATHEMATICS WORKBOOK FOR
COLLEGE ENTRANCE EXAMS
Brownstein $1.75 paper
PROFILES OF AMERICAN
COLLEGES Fine $3.95 paper
STUDENT'S RECORD BOOK:
A Record of College Years
McReynolds $1.50 paper
201 VERBS FULLY CONJUGATED IN
ALL THE TENSES   each $1.25 paper
   FRENCH Kendris SPANISH Kendris
   GERMAN Strutz   LATIN Wohlberg
VOCABULARY BUILDER
Brownstein & Weiner $1.25 paper

STEVENSON, ADLAI E., SHAPE
HISTORY; Brown $1.50
WORLD HISTORY, ESSENTIA
Smith & Smith $2.2

Barron's American an
English Classics Re-edit

BEOWULF Trans. by Thorpe $2.2
CHAUCER'S CANTERBURY T
(An Interlinear Translation)
Hopper $1.7
CLASSIC AMERICAN SHORT
STORIES Hopper   75
RASSELAS Johnson   75

Theatre Classics
for the Modern Reade

A new kind of edition of d
masterpieces in which plays
in the text as they were pr
on the stage. Illustrations c
acters and scenes, explana
staging, description of setti
costumes, full commentaries
playwrights and their plays.
    95¢ paper, $1.95 har

ALL FOR LOVE Dryden
LADY WINDERMERE'S FAN W
SHE STOOPS TO CONQUER
Goldsmith
THE BEAUX' STRATAGEM Far
THE BEGGAR'S OPERA Gay
THE DUCHESS OF MALFI Web
THE IMPORTANCE OF BEING
EARNEST Wilde
THE RIVALS Sheridan
THE SCHOOL FOR SCANDAL
THE WAY OF THE WORLD Co
VOLPONE, OR THE FOX Jonso
MEDIEVAL MYSTERIES,
MORALITIES AND INTERL
    $1.25 paper, $2.50 h
In a companion edition
DR. FAUSTUS Marlowe   5
HAMLET (First Quarto)   Sh
    $1
THE ALCHEMIST Jonson   5
THE KNIGHT OF THE BUI
PESTLE Beaumont & Fletcher
THE REHEARSAL, AND THE
Buckingham; Sheridan
THE SPANISH TRAGEDY
Kyd

BARRON'S SIMPLIFIED APPROACH

TO **Molière**

THE BLUNDERER
THE RIDICULOUS PRECIOUS LADIES
THE SCHOOL FOR HUSBANDS
THE SCHOOL FOR WIVES
DON JUAN
THE MISANTHROPE
DOCTOR IN SPITE OF HIMSELF
AMPHITRYON
THE MISER
TARTUFFE
THE WOULD-BE GENTLEMAN
THE LEARNED LADIES
THE IMAGINARY INVALID
and other major writings

By Bernard Grebanier

PROFESSOR EMERITUS,
BROOKLYN COLLEGE

BARRON'S EDUCATIONAL SERIES, INC.
WOODBURY, NEW YORK

CONTENTS

Molière

{ 1622–1673 }

THE AGE OF LOUIS XIV

Neoclassicism was the prevailing mode in the world of art from the time of the beginnings of scientific investigation early in the seventeenth century to the very brink of the French Revolution at the end of the eighteenth century. It was a movement that was both an extension of the Renaissance and a reaction against it. From the Renaissance, Neoclassicism inherited the worship of the Latin and Greek classics as models of perfection to be copied and imitated. But Neoclassicism was also a rejection of the extreme individualism in which the Renaissance had resulted; writers of this movement had little sympathy with purely personal emotional problems. For them interest centered on discovering ideal social conduct, the common basis for reasonable relationship between members of a society possessed of good sense.

The seventeenth century, which saw the establishment of Neoclassicism throughout Western Europe, was the period in which rationalism in philosophy and experimentation in natural science made their first great strides. At the opening of the century Francis Bacon, in England, had heralded the new scientific method of investigation, and by 1645 a number of his countrymen were meeting regularly for the purpose of reading

I

scientific papers. In 1662 Charles II granted them the charter for what became the Royal Society in that country. In Italy, Galileo's students set up the first scientific academy in 1657 at Florence. In France, Descartes, Pascal, and Gassendi met with similar groups. It was the century of the telescope, the reflector, the thermometer, the barometer, the pendulum clock, the astronomical observations of Kepler and Galileo, Newton's law of universal gravitation, Descartes' invention of analytical geometry, the development of calculus, Halley's study of comets, Swammerdam's invention of the science of entomology —to mention only a few of the scientific exploits of the time.

Step by step with this study of the laws of nature, philosophy advanced and changed. The *Essays* of Montaigne, widely read in France and other countries, spread a new gospel of detachment in judgment and tolerance for the beliefs of others. According to the great French essayist, philosophy should teach one not what religion to espouse but how to live intelligently. Self-examination, as it had been with Socrates, was with him the very basis of the search for truth. After him, René Descartes (1596-1650), one of the greatest of all mathematicians, applied the methods of mathematics to philosophical speculation. All truth, he insisted, must be proved, not accepted from "authorities." Beginning with the one axiom he could accept, *I think, therefore I must exist* (*Cogito ergo sum*), he proceeded to build intellectually his universe on purely mechanical grounds, from which he exempted only God and man's soul. Thomas Hobbes (1586-1679) in his *Leviathan* (1651) made perhaps the most revolutionary of all attempts to found a philosophy on our knowledge of natural science. He allowed no exceptions in applying mechanical principles to mind and matter. "All that exists," he said, "is body; all that occurs is motion." He is, thus, the father of mechanical empiricism.

Few philosophers have ever exercised the influence that John Locke (1632-1704) maintained over thinkers in the eighteenth century. His *Essay Concerning the Human Understanding* (1690) was the first searching examination into the origin of ideas. Locke repudiated the Platonic doctrine that man at birth is already supplied with certain fundamental concepts (the doctrine of "innate ideas"), and insisted that man's mind at birth is like a blank tablet (*tabula rasa*) on which experience is to write. From experience alone come the "materials of reason and knowledge," he said. Reflection, beginning with such a premise, naturally led next to an examination of social institutions, their merits and defects, and the conditions by which society can satisfactorily operate. For if experience is the source of ideas for every man, then human institutions, customs, and morals become of the gravest importance. Here we have, too, the inspiration for that "study of Mankind" (to quote the English poet Pope) which was, at the end of the century, to foment a revolution in France against the old order.

As these concepts were disseminated through Western Europe, such rationalistic and scientific thinking engendered in men a desire to understand life rationally, to interest themselves in the real and the contemporary rather than in the world of the imagination. It is this desire which is fundamental to Neoclassicism.

This Neo ("new") classicism, like its progenitors, the classics of Greece and Rome, aimed above all at clarity, lucidity, and simplicity. The mark of genius was no longer exalted inspiration, but rather restrained good sense. A typical neoclassicist was likely to be dignified rather than impassioned, clever rather than ardent.

Since clarity was desired, form became of great consideration to him. Through firmly molded form he could curb the exuberances of purely personal enthusiasms or dissatisfactions.

Since he was seeking the common denominator for all intelligent readers of his tongue, he respected conventions and standards. Correctness of style, of conduct, of ideas, and of values became paramount in his thinking. His intelligence became critical. He was on the alert for deviations from the norm of good sense in style, conduct, ideas, and social values. Hence, satire became in this age the most popular vehicle of literary expression.

The concern for form degenerated, in the hands of some neoclassicists, into an endless preoccupation with "rules." Aristotle's *Poetics,* which was devoted to the principles, not the rules, of dramatic composition, became now mistakenly the authority in the stipulation among dramatists for "the three unities." The neoclassical dramatist insisted that a play take place in one physical location, on one day, and be confined to one plot. Aristotle had, indeed, required that a drama have unity of action; but he had had nothing to say at all about unity of place; as for the unity of time, he did no more than observe that many plays deal with events which occupy about twenty-four hours. It was the commentators on the *Poetics* who were responsible for spinning out the doctrine of "the three unities." But in the Neoclassical Age, these unities were beyond challenge. Sometimes, as in the case of the time element in Corneille's *Le Cid,* the results are a strain upon credibility.

The neoclassical avoidance of the particular and the individual even affected the very language of literature. Diction became formalized in its effort to avoid vulgarity, and generalized in its effort to avoid the particular. Household words were considered too inelegant, and the names of characters in drama and fiction were transformed into florid Greek names for men and women alike.

Elegance, polish, wit—these were the new attractions that

Neoclassicism offered. The appeal of writers being to the intellect, rather than to the emotions, good taste and judgment were valued far more than profundity or great originality. Life was seen as a whole, not in moments. A man's character was delineated in terms of outstanding traits universally recognizable, not with any nuances or shadings which might mark him as peculiarly himself. It was not the writer's business, said one sturdy English neoclassicist, Samuel Johnson, to number the streaks of a tulip. Human nature was interesting only in its universal aspects.

Another distinguishing trait of the neoclassical school was the didactic purpose with which men wrote. They wrote to entertain, to be sure, but they entertained in order to teach. Such an objective was, of course, closely connected with their social-mindedness, their predilection for satire, and their interest in the universal rather than the particular.

Finally, it may be said of them that their interests were essentially urban. Nature, which was to be the nurse and teacher of the Romantic Movement, had little charm for the neoclassicist. Paris and London, to Frenchman and Englishman, were the focus of life. It was a misfortune to be compelled to live in the country, they felt, for in town there were people to talk to, to observe, to exchange ideas with. The neoclassicists were very fond of posing "nature" as the criterion for all values, but by that word they always meant *human nature*. Wild landscapes bored them; trees and gardens were charming only when laid out in symmetrical rows, clipped in geometric shapes, and approached by easy walks.

France, or, more precisely, Paris, was the capital of Neoclassicism. There are many reasons why this should have been so, but no reason is more basic than the fact that the French are classicists by temperament. The French have always delighted in logical discussion, and have always tended to intellectualize their emotions. They are naturally a critical people. Their very language reflects their passion for fine distinction and precision. It is not surprising that in this period France should have, therefore, achieved her golden age of literature. Montaigne (who was a precursor of Neoclassicism), Corneille, Racine, Molière, La Fontaine, Pascal, La Bruyère, Bossuet, Boileau, Voltaire, La Rochefoucauld, Mme de Sévigné—these are among the very greatest names in French literature, and they all belong to this period.

Louis XIV, who reigned from 1643 to 1715, the Grand Monarch, the Sun-King, had much to do with the conscious realization of French genius in his time. Under him and his absolute monarchy, France first emerged as the leading nation on the Continent. The Court became the center of national life; even the critical intelligence of Molière accepted without question the finality of the King's judgments in all matters. Louis indulged his taste for luxury, pomp, and elegance to the full. His costly palace at Versailles, with its miles of formal gardens, fountains, beautiful galleries, became the envy and model throughout Europe of royal living at its best. He gave employment to the best architects and artists of the time, and was the personal patron of some of its writers. Molière was his chief entertainer; Racine and Boileau his appointed historians; Bossuet the chaplain to his court.

MOLIÈRE'S CAREER

The greatest writer of classic comedy in Europe was born Jean-Baptiste Poquelin, but he is known to the world by his stage-name of Molière. The family Poquelin was well-established as prosperous merchants of furniture. In 1631 Molière's father bought the post of "royal upholsterer," a title that conferred much honor on this middle-class family. The boy was educated by the Jesuits at the fashionable Collège de Clermont, where his enthusiasm for Latin made him familiar with the works of the Roman comic dramatists. Some biographies are of the opinion that on leaving school, Molière studied law and practiced it for a time; it is true that his plays indicate considerable knowledge of legal matters. At any rate, it was not long before he fell in love with the stage and, discarding the reversion of the office of "royal upholsterer" and all the bright prospects therewith connected, he joined the Béjart family to form an acting troupe. They had their troubles in finding a theater; Molière, moreover, proved highly unsuited to the heavy tragic roles he had assumed. Before long the elder Poquelin was rescuing his son from debtor's prison.

With the Béjarts, nevertheless, the young man was determined to throw in his lot. For thirteen years they toured provinces, wandering from town to town, enduring every kind of hardship. But the experience proved invaluable to Molière's art as actor and playwright. The first of the plays that can be definitely ascribed to him, *The Blunderer* (*L'Étourdi*) was presented at Lyons in 1655. This play and *The Lovers' Quarrel* (*Le Dépit amoureux*) of the next year, were both written in the style of the Italians. At last acquiring the interest of the King's brother, Molière was able to realize his dream of returning to Paris. In 1658 his company presented a play of Corneille's and *Le Dépit* before the King at the Louvre. Within a week the players were granted the use of the Hôtel du Petit-Bourbon, a theater adjoining the King's palace. Here it was that Molière enjoyed his first great success, *The Ridiculous Precious Ladies* (*Les Précieuses ridicules*) in 1659. It was the right moment for the satire, and Molière's genius may be said to have come into its own with this hilarious ridicule of affectation and false elegance. At the *salon* of Mme de Rambouillet a group of elegant ladies and gentlemen had been exerting themselves to purify the French language of coarseness and vulgarity. Much of what they achieved is to their credit. But they had their inept imitators who were pushing their phraseology to the point of the absurd. It was this sham elegance which Molière pilloried in *Les Précieuses*. The satire was so brilliantly handled that it is applicable to affectation of speech in any era.

THE BLUNDERER

L'Étourdi

SCENE: *A public square in Messina*

Persons of the Drama

Lélie: *Pandolfe's son*
Célie: *Trufaldin's slave*
Mascarille: *Lélie's valet*
Hippolyte: *Anselme's daughter*
Trufaldin: *an old man*
Anselme: *Hippolyte's father*
Pandolfe: *Lélie's father*
Léandre: *a young man of rank*
Andrès: *masquerading as a gipsy*
Ergaste: *Mascarille's friend*
A Messenger; Two troupes of Masqueraders

ACT I. Lélie is upset because Léandre, a young man of rank, is his rival in affection for Célie, Trufaldin's slave. Lélie is convinced that her manner indicates she is nobly descended, and says as much to his servant Mascarille. The wily Mascarille considers his young master hopelessly romantic, and reminds him that Pandolfe, Lélie's father, has already arranged that his son marry Hippolyte, having already pledged his word to that effect to her father, Anselme. If Pandolfe ever discovers Lélie's love for Célie, there will be trouble. But all Lélie can think of is that the girl seems to favor him, despite Léandre's threats to win her. Mascarille reflects that if only Lélie had the cash, Trufaldin might be willing to sell Célie, for he worships gold. Master and man now walk over to a place beneath Célie's window. She appears briefly, but as Trufaldin's voice is heard, Mascarille bids his master conceal himself a while.

Trufaldin upbraids Célie for holding converse with Mascarille, who gives as an excuse that he has sought the girl out for her skill in fortune-telling. Mascarille continues: his master is languishing for a lovely girl, and would gladly speak of his passion, "but there is a watchful dragon who keeps watch over her." Worst of all, his master now learns, too, that he has a rival. Pretending to predict the future, Célie bids Mascarille deliver her prophecy: his master may indeed hope for success. Impatient, Lélie now re-appears and ruins everything by telling Trufaldin that he has sent Mascarille to speak with him concerning the purchase of Célie. The stories of Mascarille and Lélie cancel each other out, and, with a threat to both of them, Trufaldin chases Célie away from the window. Mascarille is annoyed at his master's clumsiness. Lélie goes off.

Old Anselme, Hippolyte's father, comes in. Mascarille approaches him and contrives that Anselme drops his purse without the old miser's noticing it. Again our blunderer ruins matters. Lélie enters, sees the purse, cries, "Whose is it?" and receives the thanks of Anselme, who pockets it again. Anselme goes off, and Mascarille berates Lélie: he had intended the money in the purse for the purchase of Célie. He has a new plan, but tells his master to disappear, after making him swear never to interfere again.

Pandolfe comes in, and begins to complain of his son. Mascarille agrees: Lélie's ill-conduct puts Mascarille out of patience. Just now they were quarreling because Mascarille was pointing out that it is Lélie's filial duty to marry Hippolyte. Pandolfe can gain his objective and end Lélie's infatuation for a certain slave by sending Anselme to buy her and thereafter ship her beyond the sea. Mascarille undertakes to resell her to the merchants. Pandolfe consents to the plan, and exits.

Hippolyte enters and scolds Mascarille: he had promised to help her in her love for Léandre and in escaping the marriage to Lélie. She is sure he is deceiving everyone, for she has overheard his words to Pandolfe. He confesses that what he wishes to do is arrange that Lélie marry Célie; that would free Hippolyte—and he has done all this scheming for Hippolyte's sake! He is offended at her ingratitude, and forgives her only when she hands him a large tip, and promises more when their plans shall have been carried out. She exits.

Lélie comes in and boasts to Mascarille that he has prevented a new catastrophe. Anselme was about to carry off Célie, when Lélie arrived in the nick of time and urged Trufaldin to keep the girl at home. Mascarille is beside himself again: it was he who talked Pandolfe into purchasing Célie; then he himself was to have been given charge of her. This settles it—Mascarille will attempt nothing more for his master. He goes off in a huff. Lélie hastens after him to conciliate him.

ACT II. Threatening to wash his hands of Lélie's love-affair if there are any more blunders, Mascarille discloses his new plan. He has floated a rumor, which came to Pandolfe's ears, that the workmen laying the foundations of Pandolfe's country house have come upon a hoard of gold. That was enough to make Pandolfe and the rest of his family run off to the country at once. Meantime, in town Mascarille has let it be known that Pandolfe has just died. Lélie fails to understand where this will lead, but he leaves that to his servant.

Mascarille now assures Anselme that his friend Pandolfe is "dead—to all intents and purposes." Lélie wishes to give his father a splendid burial—could Anselme lend him enough to defray the costs? Lélie enters weeping and Anselme gives him the sum. All the young man can do is wail, and he exits doing so. Anselme would have liked a receipt, but Mascarille protests that such crassness could not be exhibited to a youth so plunged in grief. He himself goes out wailing in sympathy.

Suddenly Pandolfe appears, very much alive. Anselme thinks him a ghost, and promises to have masses said for the dead man. But this dead man begins to laugh. Learning of his demise, Pandolfe exclaims: "What! Could I have died without knowing it?" After some persuasion Anselme accepts his friend's being still alive; he begs him to help him get his money back. Pandolfe is not interested; he goes out preoccupied with the intention of punishing Mascarille.

Lélie returns. Anselme tells him that among the coins he has just given him were some counterfeit ones he forgot to remove. Simple-minded Lélie hands back the purse, which Anselme immediately pockets, after which he harangues him for killing off his father. He leaves in indignation.

Mascarille, back, asks Lélie for the money, and learns how it has been returned. He is in a rage. Let Célie be slave or a free girl, let Léandre buy her or let her stay where she is, he is through bothering about her. Lélie pleads with him, even threatening to commit suicide there and then. Mascarille won't relent.

Trufaldin and Léandre enter, whispering. Taking pity on his master, Mascarille pushes him off, and promises to help. Trufaldin takes leave of Léandre, who soliloquizes on his joy in finding a way to be sure of having Célie.

Mascarille comes in running and shouting: "Help! Murder!" Lélie, he says, has just beaten him two hundred times with a cudgel. He vows vengeance. Léandre quiets him and offers to employ him. Mascarille accepts with alacrity, and is ready to help him to Célie. No need of that, says Léandre: he has just purchased her at a low price. But he must be careful that his father does not learn of the transaction: therefore he has dealt with Trufaldin in someone else's name. Léandre's ring is to be the token of recognition; on sight of it, Trufaldin is to hand over Célie. Now Léandre seeks a place to hide the girl; Mascarille offers a little house just out of town belonging to an old relation of his. Delighted, Léandre gives him the ring and asks him to deliver Célie to that house.

Just then Hippolyte comes in, tells Léandre she has news for him, and walks off with him. Alone, Mascarille exults in the thought that his master is about to come to felicity through the help of his rival! Trufaldin enters, sees the ring, and is about to fetch Célie, when a messenger arrives with a letter for him. It is from the Marquis of Montalcana, who has just learned that his daughter, stolen from him when she was four, is now Trufaldin's slave, Célie. The Marquis will arrive soon, and will greatly recompense Trufaldin for his trouble. Trufaldin announces that Mascarille had better tell his employer that the sale of Célie will not take place.

Lélie now triumphantly informs Mascarille that, having heard that Léandre had purchased Célie, he has written a letter feigning it came from a grandee, Célie's father, who would reward Trufaldin: the stratagem has worked well— Trufaldin will not hand over Célie to Léandre. As Lélie is crowing with delight over his talents, the exasperated servant admits himself unequal to the praises Lélie merits, and dashes out, once more furious with his blundering master.

ACT III. Mascarille will try a new scheme—not for his master's sake, but for the honor of carrying out purposes begun. If only he could get Lélie out of the way a bit! Léandre enters; he has heard of Lélie's letter, knows who wrote it, but is annoyed that Trufaldin still believes it. So much smitten with Célie, Léandre thinks, slave though she is, he will marry her. Mascarille tells him that if he knew all the facts he would alter his intentions: she has been free with her favors all over town. Léandre is incredulous, Mascarille indifferent. What is it to him? "Marry her. The whole town will thank you." Shocked, Léandre sends Mascarille off on a commission, crushed at his having been taken in by the girl.

Lélie enters; Léandre confesses his folly in loving a girl of such easy virtue. Incensed, Lélie defends her and is ready to fight. Léandre is firm: his informant is a reliable source, Mascarille. In a towering rage, Lélie bets Léandre that he will make Mascarille eat his words: "I will cudgel him to death if he dare utter such lies to me." LÉANDRE: "And I will cut his ears off if he doesn't stand by every words he said to me."

Mascarille comes back; Lélie begins to abuse him, paying no heed to the other's warning whispers and winks. Unable to make him repeat his scurrilous report of Célie, Lélie draws his sword and threatens to kill him. Léandre intervenes. LÉLIE: "What's wrong? Can't I correct my own servant?" LÉANDRE: "What do you mean—*your* servant?" The argument takes a new turn. Mascarille is now in his employ, Léandre avers, since Lélie gave him that terrible drubbing. Mascarille tries to save the situation, but Léandre sees the light, realizes he has been imposed upon, and leaves. Once more Mascarille lets his master know how he has ruined all. He concludes: "You'll never be anything but an ass while you've any breath left in you." He sends Lélie out to placate PANDOLFE: "I killed him this morning for your sake. . . . Your good father, old as he is, loves life immensely." In dread of Pandolfe's anger, Mascarille is tempted to seek refuge in jail. As his master exits, Mascarille is glad of a breathing-space while they rest from intrigue.

Ergaste, his friend, comes in to tell him that Léandre has arranged to abduct Célie, and plans to get into Trufaldin's by masquerading as a woman. Mascarille decides to benefit his master with a new trick: he will be ahead of Léandre in masking himself as a woman.

Ergaste next tells Lélie of Léandre's scheme. Lélie will have an exploit of his own. He calls up to Trufaldin and warns him to lock his doors: certain gallants are coming tonight to carry off Célie.

Trufaldin comes down into the street, just in time to greet Mascarille and friends, all masked. Thinking to tease Léandre, Lélie professes to find the masked woman attractive, while Trufaldin locks his doors against her. Mascarille removes his mask; Lélie sees it is he, not Léandre. Again Mascarille gives his master up, and goes off fuming with his friends. Léandre and his crowd come in as masked women too; Trufaldin, forewarned, greets them by dumping ordure over them from the window.

ACT IV. Lélie is now disguised as an Armenian, in accordance with Mascarille's newest device. The latter has told Trufaldin that he is weary of the world's wickedness; out of concern for his soul's health, he wishes to be near some good man and there pass the rest of his life; he desires nothing better than to live as a servant of Trufaldin's, without a penny's pay. Moreover, he will place in Trufaldin's hands a legacy left him by his father plus what he has been able to save himself; if he dies, Trufaldin will be his sole heir.

It is some time since Trufaldin left Naples, where he was called Zanobio Ruberti, Mascarille continues. Forced to quit that city suddenly by night because of certain circumstances, he left behind a wife and a very young daughter. Later he learned they were both dead; his son, Horace, was under the tutelage of a scholar at Bologna. Trufaldin wrote to Bologna, but receiving no word from son or teacher, believed them dead too, and came to Messina, where he changed his name. It is twelve years since he has heard from them. Now, Mascarille continues, Lélie is to be an Armenian merchant who has seen them both safe and sound in Turkey. (Mascarille got this idea from a recent dream which Trufaldin recounted, assuring him his son Horace was alive.) Our Armenian merchant had heard that son and tutor were living as slaves, and gave them the money to buy their freedom. Horace had asked the Armenian to visit Trufaldin and stay with him until Horace could arrive. Mascarille coaches his master in what he is to say in order to make all these inventions convincing; Lélie need not fear discovery because of his beard and exotic garb.

Trufaldin comes in and thanks Heaven for this favorable turn of fate. But he feels there is something familiar about this Armenian. Lélie overplays his part: Horace, he says, described his father just as he looks now. TRUFALDIN: "How was that possible? He was seven when he saw me last." Trufaldin asks where the Armenian met his son and the tutor recently. LÉLIE: "In Turkey at Turin." TRUFALDIN: "Turin? I thought that was in Piedmont." Mascarille quickly interjects: "You didn't understand. He means Tunis." Armenians, he explains,

habitually pronounce *Tunis* to sound like *Turin*. When Trufaldin asks for more details, Lélie goes tongue-tied. His
servant leaps to the rescue: "Ah! Signore Zanobio Ruberti,
what a joy is this sent you by Heaven!" At which Lélie remarks inanely, "Yes, Ruberti is Trufaldin's true name." Mascarille goes on to speak of Naples as Ruberti's native town,
and Lélie echoes that fact, too. Trufaldin invites the Armenian
into his house, and Mascarille's purpose is thus achieved—to
afford the lovers a chance to talk to each other.

Anselme and Léandre enter. The old man does his best
to talk his son out of his infatuation with Célie: a wife without a dowry can bring only unhappiness with her. Léandre
says he is trying to master his passion for her. They go out
as Lélie and Mascarille enter. Lélie has been ruining things
again. In Trufaldin's house he has openly demonstrated his
love for Célie by his looks and conduct. Trufaldin enters and
asks for a word alone with Mascarille, to whom he declares
that he has cut a stout cudgel which he intends for Mascarille's back as well as this counterfeit Armenian's; Trufaldin's godchild was present while Lélie was recounting to
Célie his deception of Trufaldin. Mascarille disclaims any part
in the trick; Trufaldin challenges him to prove his innocence
by helping him thrash Lélie. Lélie is called out, and Trufaldin
begins beating him; compelled to cooperate, Mascarille has
to beat his master too, but tries, at the same time, to push him
off-stage. He follows Trufaldin into the house. Lélie returns
and vows vengeance against Mascarille. From a window his
servant lets him know how he gave their plot away before
the child. He promises to aid Lélie only if he will forswear
retaliation for his beating and will take an oath never to meddle in future plans. Lélie goes off.

Ergaste relates to Mascarille a piece of bad news. A young
gypsy, of suspiciously gentlemanly air, has arrived in town

with an old woman—his purpose, to purchase Célie. This must be the admirer, Mascarille thinks, of whom Célie has spoken. What ill luck! Just as Léandre has renounced his suit of Célie and is ready to marry Hippolyte, a new rival pops up! Well, at least, a little time can be gained. A serious robbery has just been committed; gypsies are always the first to be thought guilty of theft, and Mascarille will see to it that this young gypsy is jailed for a few days.

ACT V. Mascarille is beside himself: just as the gypsy was being taken into custody, Lélie gallantly came to the rescue and helped him escape. Another device ruined!

There is a well-furnished house on this square, and it is at Mascarille's disposal. He tacks up a To Let sign on it.

The young gypsy, Andrès, is speaking to Célie. Out of love for her he has come all this way to Messina to buy her freedom, which transaction he has just completed. He is disturbed to find her looking so sad, but prepared to do anything she wishes. She pleads a headache, and asks that they postpone quitting Messina for a few days.

Mascarille, disguised as a Swiss and speaking with a strange accent, announces to Andrès that he is the master of this furnished house, and can accommodate Célie and Andrès with lodgings. Andrès leads Célie into their temporary abode. Just as he comes out again to fetch the old woman who accompanied him to Messina, Lélie sees him, and tells him that this house belongs to Lélie's father. Andrès bids him read the To Let sign. Lélie at once suspects this to be part of some new design of Mascarille to help him in his love affair. Andrès asks the name of Lélie's beloved. Learning it, Andrès promises to investigate the matter, since he has just purchased Célie himself.

Mascarille enters, still the Swiss. His master recognizes

him, but he insists that Lélie is mistaken until the latter assures him that the disguise is no longer necessary. Under some obligation to Lélie because of the rescue, Andrès is to be the author of Lélie's happiness, and will give Célie to him. The gypsy brings out Célie and asks Lélie whether it is truly reasonable to expect him, despite his indebtedness to Lélie, to sacrifice his love for anyone so beautiful. "You're generous yourself, but you would never do such a thing." As Andrès goes out, Mascarille is again in a pet. He sarcastically congratulates Lélie for having solved the problem so well.

Hippolyte and Célie converse, the former expressing her appreciation of Célie's beauty, even though it made Léandre for a time forget his obligations. Mascarille comes in breathless with a wealth of news. Andrès and Trufaldin, running to see what a great brawl in town was all about, found it had centered about the old gypsy-woman and another old dame, the latter of whom, upon seeing Trufaldin, hailed him as Ruberti. When he left Naples it was she who had charge of his daughter; the gypsy-woman was the one who had stolen the child when but four years old. Ruberti's wife died of grief soon thereafter, and the child's nurse spread the rumor that both mother and daughter were dead. While the old woman was telling this story, Andrès changed color many times, whenever the name of Ruberti was uttered. The young man at length embraced Trufaldin as his father, and revealed himself to be the long-lost Horace. Upon the death of his tutor, Horace left Bologna, wandered about to see the world for six years, and eventually came to Naples to find his kinsfolk, but in vain. Célie was now clearly identified as the lost daughter of Trufaldin-Ruberti, and Andrès as her brother. Now there can be no impediment from him to Lélie's love of Célie.

The others come in, rejoice in their discovery of their relationship, and Andrès expresses delight in having found a sister in Célie. Trufaldin gives his consent to her marrying Lélie, and Mascarille asks his master whether he could not find some new blunder with which to annihilate this solidly based success. Hippolyte and Léandre will marry, everyone is contented—has no one a wench for Mascarille? Anselme promises to arrange that he have a sweetheart, too, and Mascarille concludes with a prayer to Heaven to give them all children of which the husbands will be the true fathers.

◆   This verse comedy was based upon an Italian original by Niccolò Barbieri, its characters and complications clearly influenced by the traditions of the *commedia dell' arte*. In such a play no one looked for any depth of characterization or great consistency in the story. But the work needs no apology. Brought back from his wanderings in the provinces, *The Blunderer,* first presented at Lyons (probably in 1655), was presented by Molière in Paris in November, 1658. The play had a great success, which it has not since lost. It is a work, as Pierre Brisson has said, "conceived, written, put forth *for and by* an actor; in the role of Mascarille Molière exhibited endless resources as a comedian.

The play has its particular interest, also, as an indication more or less of the style in which Molière was to continue to work—with increasing brilliance.

THE LOVERS' QUARREL

But his next play, to be presented at Paris, in December 1658, *The Lovers' Quarrel,* earned a greater success than it merited. This five-act verse comedy is notably inferior to *The Blunderer*; its Mascarille is crafty, and takes with too much humility the beatings administered to him. The plot comes from a very complicated comedy of Nicolò Secchi, and Molière has complicated it even more. Albert is anxious to inherit his uncle's estate, which stipulates that he must himself have a son. When his wife presents him with a second daughter, Dorothée, he exchanges her for an infant boy, Ascagne, whose mother sells flowers. The boy dies after ten months during Albert's absence, and Albert's wife substitutes her own daughter. Without his knowledge, therefore, Dorothée is raised as his son, under the name of Ascagne. When his wife dies, the secret is buried with her. It is when Dorothée-Ascagne is a young woman-man that a series of incredible complexities due to love begin.

THE RIDICULOUS
PRECIOUS LADIES

Les Précieuses ridicules

SCENE: *Gorgibus' house in Paris*

Persons of the Drama

La Grange ⎱
Du Croisy ⎰ *repulsed lovers*
Gorgibus: *a good citizen*
The Marquis de Mascarille: *valet to La Grange*
The Viscount Jodelet: *valet to Du Croisy*
Almanzor: *footman to the precious ladies*
Two Chairmen
Musicians
Madelon: *daughter to Gorgibus* ⎱ *the ridiculous*
Cathos: *niece to Gorgibus* ⎰ *precious ladies*
Marotte: *maid to the ridiculous precious ladies*
Lucile ⎱
Célimène ⎰ *two female neighbors*

La Grange and Du Croisy [Molière employed the names
of two actors actually in his troupe] are outraged at the treat-

22

ment they have just received at the hands of Madelon and Cathos, respectively the daughter and niece of Gorgibus. They were treated to the greatest rudeness of manner and abruptness of speech by these pretentious girls. It was too much to see a couple of country wenches giving themselves such airs. Affectation has spread from Paris even into the country, like a disease. La Grange is resolved to teach the girls a lesson in distinguishing the cultivated from the low. He has a valet, Mascarille, who has taken it into his head to ape the manners of the nobility. He prides himself on his gallantry and verse, and looks down his nose at his fellow-servants. La Grange is going to use him for an exploit he has in mind. The two rejected suitors go out just as Gorgibus comes in. He notices the annoyance on their faces.

Gorgibus summons the girls and asks them why La Grange and Du Croisy have left so disgruntled; Madelon and Cathos must know that these men are destined to be their husbands. Madelon complains that they had been coarse enough to propose marriage. What's wrong with that? Gorgibus wants to know. Good grief! exclaims Madelon: if everybody was as inelegant as her father love-stories would soon be over. "A lover, to be acceptable, must know how to utter fine sentiments, to breathe soft, tender, and ardent vows; his courtship must follow the rules." He ought first to see his beloved at some public place, like a church; when he leaves her he should be melancholy; when visiting her he should for a while conceal his passion. When he at last makes his declaration—preferably in some garden-walk—he should at once become angry. After a brief banishment, he finds a way to pacify the beloved until she grows used to hearing his passion. After that come: rivals, persecution of fathers, baseless jealousies, etc., etc. But to come out point-blank and propose marriage is to begin the novel at the end—it is sickening!

Gorgibus considers all this to be undecipherable nonsense. Cathos adds that their suitors seem painfully unfamiliar with the fashionable writings on gallantry: they have no ornaments on their legs, no feathers in their hats, only a few ribbons on their coats. Gorgibus thinks both girls are mad; he is upset that they have changed their names to the cultivated ones of Aminta and Polixena. They protest that their given names would disgrace the best novel in the world.

He is determined that they shall marry the men he has chosen for them. Cathos considers marriage shocking: "How can one stand the thought of lying at the side of a man who is thoroughly naked?" Madelon asks for some time before marriage to become familiar with the fashionable world of Paris. Gorgibus goes out threatening them that they will be married by the end of the year or else become nuns.

The servant comes in to say that a footman has arrived to announce the coming of his master, the Marquis de Mascarille. The girls are delighted, and rush off to re-arrange their hair.

Two men come in bearing a sedan-chair with Mascarille. They have to threaten to beat him before he agrees to pay them. The girls come back and Mascarille begins to assault them with extravagant compliments couched in the most outrageously artificial style. The girls try to match him; calling for some chairs, Madelon asks the servant to bring in "the conveniences of conversation." They all agree that "outside of Paris there is no salvation for the fashionable world." Mascarille promises to introduce the girls to the best society: "I will establish an academy of wits at your house, and I promise you that not a line of poetry shall be written in Paris but what you shall have memorized before anyone else." He himself, when in the humor, composed many hundreds of songs, sonnets, and epigrams, and a thousand madrigals. At present he is engaged "in turning all of Roman history into madrigals." He now treats them to some idiotic verses he composed yesterday at the house of a duchess, with the concluding line, "Stop thief! stop thief! stop thief!" Then he goes over it again, phrase by phrase, inviting their admiration of every detail. They are happy to oblige. Then he offers to sing the melody he wrote for the poem. He never studied music, but "people of rank know everything without having had to learn anything." After his singing, he again points out to their enthusiastic ears the merits of his song.

The girls complain of their life. He undertakes to escort them to see a new comedy.

What do they think of the decorations, rosettes and ribbons of his clothes? They look, says Madelon, "furiously well." MASCARILLE: "Please to concentrate the reflection of your faculty for smelling upon these gloves of mine." CATHOS: "I never inhaled a more delicious perfume." He asks them to sniff at his powdered wig. MADELON: "It titillates the nerves of the upper region most delightfully."

Suddenly Mascarille cries out "Murder" upon the girls; both of them have smitten his heart and the contest is too unequal and unfair. MADELON: "He is a consummate wit."

Now the Viscount de Jodelet is announced, an intimate friend of the Marquis. The girls are in heaven at the thought that people of quality are finding their way to this house. JODELET: "Your charms demand their lordly rights from all sorts of people." The two men outdo each other before the girls in giving each other a fine reputation as great leaders of armies. They suggest having the musicians in so that the four may dance; the girls agree and send for the servants in order to fill up the numbers for a dance.

The Marquis and Viscount begin to lead them in a Coranto—which proves a little too fast for them to manage gracefully. In the midst of the dance Du Croisy and La Grange come in, cudgels in hand, and proceed to beat the Viscount and Marquis for pretending to be men of rank. The spurned lovers go out.

The sham noblemen pretend that their beating was only a wager, and urge the girls to continue the dance. Du Croisy and La Grange come in again. Madelon demands the reason of this intrusion. DU CROISY: "Shall we permit our footmen to be received better than ourselves?" The girls are shocked to learn that the Marquis and Viscount are only servants, dressed up in their masters' clothes. The rejected lovers go out again.

Gorgibus re-enters to denounce the girls for the mess they have got into. He approves of the revenge taken by the suitors. The girls order the false noblemen to leave at once. MASCARILLE: "Is this the way to treat a marquis?" Gorgibus commands the girls to keep out of his sight. The curtain goes down on his soliloquy: "And you, the cause of their folly, you romances, verses, songs, sonnets, and sonatas—may the Devil take the lot of you!"

◆ This one-act prose comedy of 1659 discovered for Molière his true bent. It is a fountain of high spirits and hilarity. The public adored it, though the world of fashion resented the fidelity of its satire. But Molière had won the favor of the King. Saintsbury says of this little gem: "In its way it has never been surpassed either as a piece of social criticism or a piece of brilliant dialogue illustrating action and character."

SGANARELLE

Molière next wrote Sganarelle, or the Imaginary Cuckold (1660), a farce, which introduces what was to become a favor-

ite character of the dramatist, the cowardly Sganarelle of
the title. Sganarelle, good Parisian bourgeois, thinks he is being deceived by his wife because he has found her kissing a
miniature of Lélie, Célie's young lover. This is enough to lead
into all sorts of complications, skillfully contrived by the
dramatist. Lélie also becomes involved in them when he sees
his own portrait in the hands of Sganarelle, who has taken
it away from his wife; Lélie concludes that Sganarelle had it
from Célie, Lélie's betrothed. Everything turns out all right
and the lovers marry; Sganarelle speaks the moral of the farce:
"Did anyone ever do a better job than I in thinking himself
cuckolded? You may gather from this that the strongest of
appearances may hurl the mind into the falsest credulity."

Sganarelle will re-appear in *The School for Husbands,
The Forced Marriage, Don Juan* and *Doctor in Spite of Himself*. He is a type, but less of a clown than Mascarille and
more human. As Des Granges described him, Sganarelle is
"sometimes the bourgeois grumbler and fool, authoritarian
and narrow-minded; sometimes the chicken-hearted valet,
cowardly, gluttonous; sometimes the drunk and brutal peasant,
but clever and wily."

Sganarelle was enormously popular in Paris before it was
ever presented at court. Nevertheless, it is no longer thought
to be among its author's finest works. At the moment he
seems to have had neither satirical nor didactic purposes. On
October 11, 1660 the Théâtre du Petit Bourbon, where Molière's company had been performing, was demolished by the
Superintendent of Works. No advance warning had been
given the troupe, and the machinery housed in the old theatre
was destroyed, too. The King gave Molière the Salle du Palais
Royal to perform in. But the rival theatre, the Hôtel de
Bourgogne, saw an opportunity to undo Molière by trying to
incorporate in its numbers his troupe; but his actors were too

much devoted to him to be thus seduced away from their leader.

DON GARCIA OF NAVARRE

When the Palais Royal was ready for the company, Molière early in 1661 presented a five-act verse tragi-comedy—for him, an amazingly heavy piece—which was a total failure, *Don Garcia of Navarre or The Jealous Prince*. The disfavor with which the piece met was somewhat owing to Molière's inadequate performance in it, for he seems to have been unsuited to tragic roles; indeed his seriousness in the role of Don Garcia caused much mirth in the theatre. But that was owing, too, to the demands of the tragic style prevalent in that day—exaggerations of voice and gesture of which Molière was incapable. "Nature," records La Serre, "had been so generous in equipping him with a lively, witty genius" that he was not presentable in grave roles. The hero of this play, a fanciful prince, is ever the victim of unreasonable and unjustified jealousy—a man of childishly bad temper. The heroine is incredibly patient with him, and she herself sounds too much like those very *précieuses* whom Molière had ridiculed.

THE SCHOOL FOR HUSBANDS

Sganarelle appears again in a verse comedy, first performed on June 24, 1661, *The School for Husbands*. Taking a hint from Terence's *Adelphi,* where we find two old men of opposite dispositions, one a father, the other an uncle, giving very different educations to their respective son and nephew, Molière presents us with two guardians, each responsible for the rearing of one of two sisters, one man being inflexible, the other indulgent. Molière adds the interest of making these men troubled not only with fatherly concern but with the problems of lovers, too. Voltaire had the greatest admiration for this play.

THE SCHOOL FOR HUSBANDS

L'École des maris

SCENE: *A public place in Paris*

Persons of the Drama

Sganarelle ⎫
Ariste ⎬ *brothers*
Valère: *lover to Isabelle*
Ergaste: *servant to Valère*
A Magistrate
A Notary
Isabelle ⎫
Léonor ⎬ *sisters*
Lisette: *maid to Isabelle*

Sganarelle and his elder brother, Ariste, have the guardian-ship of two orphan sisters, Isabelle and Léonor. Sganarelle, who thinks well of himself, expects to marry Isabelle.

ACT I. Sganarelle is being upbraided by his elder brother Ariste for shunning the pleasures of society and dressing and living as though he were uncivilized, but defends his right to do without all the extravagances of fashion. Ariste does not recommend dressing like a fop, he insists, but merely not looking like an eccentric: "both extremes are offensive; in his apparel as well as in his speech, every wise man should not be affected, but be ready for the changes of custom." Sganarelle mocks his brother for trying to conceal grey hairs under a black wig—and at his age! Ariste is tired of always being reminded of his age, as though it were a crime for old people to be cheerful; old age has inconveniences enough without being condemned to think always of the grave.

While Ariste and Sganarelle continue talking at one end of the stage, Léonor, her waiting woman Lisette, and Isabelle come in without seeing them. Poor Isabelle complains of being usually kept locked up all day by her guardian; Léonor is lucky to be the ward of a rational man. Sganarelle intercepts them and refuses to allow Isabelle to take a walk with her sister. Ariste pleads for her in vain; his brother resents the intrusion. He accuses Ariste of encouraging Léonor in idleness, in gadding about, and flirting with dandies; if that's the way Ariste wishes to bring up his ward, let him. As for himself, he intends to make Isabelle dress soberly, stay within doors, and concern herself with domestic matters; he intends to marry her and he wants to be sure of having the kind of wife who suits him. He chides Léonor as a bad influence on her sister; the girl retorts that Sganarelle's conduct is not such as to inspire love in Isabelle. Honor must be weak that requires policing, and no precautions can prevent a girl from carrying out her wishes. Ariste upholds Léonor's arguments, to his brother's annoyance. The father of the girls in his will signified his desire that Isabelle marry Sganarelle and Léonor, Ariste; but Ariste has no intention of forcing Léonor to marry him. All Ariste wishes is his ward's happiness. Sganarelle warns his brother that if Ariste should marry Léonor he will have to pay for having allowed her too much freedom—their house will be filled with young suitors. Sganarelle chases Isabelle back into the house. Alone, Sganarelle soliloquizes on his brother's condition: "A foolish old man with a worn-out body who plays the fop, a girl-sweetheart who is a thorough coquette, and impudent servants." He himself plans to send Isabelle off to the country.

Valère and his servant Ergaste enter. Wishing to strike up an acquaintance with Sganarelle, Valère bows politely, and introduces himself as a neighbor. He invites Sganarelle to interest himself in the attractions of Paris and suggests dropping in to see him. But his neighbor Sganarelle is ill-mannered, cuts him short, and exits. Valère is in a rage: Isabelle, whom he loves, is "in the power of a savage, a watchful dragon," who will not allow her a moment's liberty. Ergaste reflects that that kind of supervision always makes a woman ready to yield to an admirer: Sganarelle's surliness must be therefore considered an advantage to Valère. But the lover has had no opportunity to plead his cause; he does not even know whether Isabelle is aware of his feelings. The two men go out.

ACT II. Isabelle has directed her guardian to Valère's house; she has some sort of plan in view. He knocks at the door; Valère and his servant come out. The young man invites Sganarelle in; he refuses. Valère next offers to have a chair brought; he rejects that offer, too. Does Valère know that he is Isabelle's guardian? Yes. Does he also know that since Sganarelle finds her charming, he destines her to be his own wife? No! Well, now Valère knows, and he is to leave Isabelle in peace. How has Sganarelle learned of Valère's affection? the young man asks. From Isabelle herself. "Virtuous girl, that she is, who has loved me from childhood, she has just told me all." Moreover, she bade her guardian tell him that she is well aware of Valère's passion; since she has no other means of communication, she asks her guardian to transmit the message that her love is denied to all save Sganarelle. Valère is not sure of how to take this news, and retires. Alone, Sganarelle congratulates himself on his ward's virtuous conduct.

Afraid that Valère may misinterpret her intent, Isabelle comes out again. She tells her guardian that she fears their troubles are not over. From her window just now she beheld Valère's emissary, who proceeded to throw her a box, which no doubt contains a love-letter. The only thing to do is to have the box re-delivered to the sender. She herself is not in a position to bring it back, and confides it to Sganarelle's care. But he must not open it, lest Valère imagine she was interested enough to read his message. Chortling with delight at his success in raising his ward—"I'd like to know if my brother's ward would have acted thus!"— Sganarelle delivers the box to Ergaste, with the warning that his master is to trouble Isabelle with no more letters. Sganarelle goes home.

Valère opens the box and reads the letter. In it Isabelle speaks of her misery at the imminence of her marriage to Sganarelle, six days hence. It is her despair which makes her thus reckless. Only Valère can rescue her. Her lover feels that his affection is doubled by this tender note. Sganarelle comes out again, and cries to Valère: "You see how your presents are received! You're wasting your ammunition, I assure you. Isabelle is a discreet girl. She loves me and your suit is an insult to her." Valère feigns that he is convinced, and apologizes. If he had had any idea that Sganarelle was the favored man, he would never have tried competing against his superior. As a last kindness he asks Sganarelle to transmit to the girl a message affirming the purity of his love and his having desired to make her his wife, and the permanence of his love for her. Only his respect for Sganarelle's merits could check his suit of her. SGANARELLE: "This is wisely said."

Sganarelle now reports to Isabelle Valère's grief and final message. Sganarelle finds himself pitying the youth. But the delighted Isabelle pretends to be outraged by Valère, and is annoyed at her guardian's pity. Will not Valère try to carry her off by force? So she has been told. It is all Sganarelle's fault for not having been sharp with the young man; Valère still thinks she loves him and that she dreads marrying her guardian. He was only making sport of Sganarelle. Sganarelle is shocked. His ward bids him speak to Valère again, tell him that Isabelle knows of the planned abduction, and that he should not require being told the same thing twice. Sganarelle is still more delighted with her loyalty.

At Valère's door, Sganarelle delivers his message. He adds that, lest the young man think *he* has invented Isabelle's words, he is free to come and hear her speak them herself.

Isabelle pretends anger at having to see Valère. Sganarelle explains that he simply wishes her to tell the young man how much she hates him. ISABELLE: (*to* VALÈRE) "Have I not completely bared my soul to your eyes, and are you still in doubt whom I love?" VALÈRE: "Your final verdict, which must decide the fate of my great love, moves me so greatly that you cannot be offended if I desire to have it repeated." ISABELLE: "I have sufficiently made plain my real feelings. I have suffered too long this terrible torture. The man I love must be diligent to make the man I hate abandon all hope, and must deliver me by a happy marriage from a wretchedness worse than death." While pretending to embrace Sganarelle she gives Valère her hand to kiss. Sganarelle asks Valère whether the girl has not been clear enough. VALÈRE: "Well, madam, . . . your words tell me what you would have me do. I shall soon find a way to rid you of the one who so greatly offends you." Sganarelle still pities Valère so much that in compassion he embraces him.

ACT III. Sganarelle is surprised to see Isabelle leaving the house; she had asked to be allowed to remain in her room undisturbed. Isabelle confides: alas! Léonor has developed a passion for Valère, and Isabelle has shut her up in her room. Imagine the extent of Léonor's delirium that she should have come alone here at this hour to confess to her sister that this love-affair has been going on for a year. Léonor says she will die if Valère goes away; she has begged her sister to allow her to masquerade as Isabelle and meet Valère at night in the street so that she may somehow coax him into staying in Paris. Isabelle has upbraided Léonor for allowing herself to love a man so fickle, but Léonor's passion is too great. Sganarelle is against all this mystery's going on in his house, and wishes to send Léonor away. Well, if Sganarelle insists—! But let him conceal himself, and let Léonor go away without his speaking to her. Sganarelle can hardly wait for the next day to inform his brother and gloat over the mess he has made of educating *his* ward. Isabelle goes out, and we hear her offstage telling her sister that she must leave at once. She comes out again, disguised as her sister. Sure that Léonor is going to meet Valère, Sganarelle follows the girl.

He hears her tell Valère that she is Isabelle, mutters that she is a liar, and sees Valère conduct her into the latter's house. In order to save Léonor's honor, Sganarelle is determined that the girl now housed with Valère must marry the young man, and therefore raps on the door of a magistrate. Luckily there is also a notary at the judge's quarters. Sganarelle also knocks at Ariste's door. SGANARELLE: "Come, my fine teacher, . . . I've something lovely to show you." He delivers a sermon to his elder brother for being a superannuated fool who has only encouraged Léonor in vice by his lenient ways; Ariste finds it hard to believe that, as he is told, Léonor is really in love with Valère and is now in Valère's house.

In the meantime the Magistrate and the Notary have been interviewing Isabelle in Valère's house; the Magistrate comes out to say that no forced marriage will be necessary. Both parties are ready to tie the knot. Valère appears at a window and says that no one will enter until he knows what is intended. He himself has already signed the marriage contract. If his elders approve of this marriage, they must sign their names, too. Sganarelle, sure that the bride-to-be is Léonor masquerading as Isabelle (and that Valère has no idea whom he is really marrying), and Ariste, who in any case will not stand in the way of Léonor's choice, both sign the document. The Magistrate and Notary re-enter the house; Sganarelle and his brother retire to the back of the stage.

Léonor comes in with Lisette. Ariste's ward has found the ball dreary and has left it; she is bored to death with the young fops she knows. For her part, she values much more the love of an old man than the ardors of these giddy youths. Ariste comes forward and gently reproves Léonor: he is hurt, after all his indulgence, that she has acted so secretively, especially after professing her love for him. She does not understand; it would seem a crime to her to love anyone else but him.

Just then all the others come out of Valère's house. Isabelle asks her sister's forgiveness for having used her name to further her own love. To her guardian she does not apologize, since they were never made for each other. Now that the facts are plain, Ariste urges his brother to accept them quietly. Sganarelle is himself responsible for the way things turned out. Ergaste thinks him lucky: had he married he must have been cuckolded. But Sganarelle renounces "the treacherous sex" forever. Lisette has the play's last line, addressed to the audience: "If you know of any churlish husbands, be sure to send them to school with us."

◆ It is interesting to recollect that Molière himself enacted the role of Sganarelle. This play seems to have been the first ever written with "The School for" as part of the title. Its success canceled the setback Molière suffered with *Don Garcia*. Henceforth his career was assured. It marks an important advance, too, in Molière's career as a dramatist. Here the situations seem to arise from the temperament of the characters for the first time, instead of being inventions to move a plot. Here, as well, one finds the two-fold purpose of his greatest plays: to amuse and to instruct. In *The School for Husbands* the dramatist warns against the folly of governing by restraint instead of by moral force. But Sganarelle is by no means a clown; he is rather the victim of a defect of character which is ridiculed, and at the end is somewhat pathetic.

The English dramatist Wycherley wrote *The Country Wife* (1672) in partial imitation of *The School for Husbands*. Lesser English dramatists have also freely adapted it, in whole or in part.

THE BORES

It is obvious that in *The School for Husbands* the author was expressing his own convictions in the person of Ariste. About eight months after the performance of this play, Molière contracted a most unfortunate marriage with Armande Béjart (February 20, 1662), who was twenty-one years his junior. She was a sister of Madeleine Béjart of the troupe, and proved a heartless coquette.

Projected, written, completed, rehearsed, and ready for performance all in two weeks, *The Bores* (*Les Facheux*) a verse comedy in three acts was first acted at Vaux, the seat of the Superintendent of Finances, on August 17, 1661 before the King and the Court (the Queen alone not being present). Three weeks later the Superintendent of Finances, Fouquet, was arrested, and shut up in prison for the rest of his life. The comedy was not played in Paris until November.

In his Preface Molière says: "There was never a dramatic performance so hurried as this one . . . [I say this] only to prevent the objections of certain people that I have not presented all the kinds of bores to be found." If the pressure of time was responsible for his choosing only a small number, it was all the more daring of him to limit himself, as he did, to the types of bores who were in fashion at Court. But the King was delighted with this piece, in which scenes and portraits follow one another without much attempt at connecting them. We meet the gambler, the braggart huntsman, the pedant, the little Marquis, the dancer, the duelist, etc.

THE SCHOOL FOR WIVES

In 1662, some ten months after his own marriage, Molière wrote one of his most important comedies, in verse, *The School for Wives,* a fine study of incompatibility in marriage. It was presented on December 26, 1662. Louis XIV was so much impressed that Molière was granted a royal pension.

It followed by a year and a half *The School for Husbands,* and was no doubt suggested by it. The two plays have more than a little in common: the jealous and arbitrary lover, in a position of authority over the girl he loves; and the young ward who is rescued from an odious marriage by the ingenuities of young love. Arnolphe is something like Sganarelle, but more refined and certainly less odious. He also more dominates his play, rarely quitting the scene. Agnès is a simple girl at first, but her character develops with the progress of the plot.

It is hard to resist the conviction that the writing of this play was owing to Molière's having already learned, from his brief experience of marriage with his flirtatious wife, the pangs of jealousy. There is more than a little of bitterness and passion in the utterances of Arnolphe, and it is as though the dramatist found some relief from his anguish in castigating himself in the person of Arnolphe and in depicting his absurdities.

THE SCHOOL FOR WIVES

L'École des femmes

SCENE: *A square in a city*

Persons of the Drama

Arnolphe: *alias M. de la Souche*
Chrysalde: *friend to Arnolphe*
Horace: *in love with Agnès*
Enrique: *brother-in-law of Chrysalde*
Oronte: *father to Horace and a great friend to Arnolphe*
Alain: *a country fellow, servant to Arnolphe*
A Notary
Agnès: *a young innocent girl, brought up by Arnolphe*
Georgette: *a country-woman, servant to Arnolphe*

ACT I. Arnolphe tells his friend, Chrysalde, that he intends getting married tomorrow. Chrysalde is worried: hundreds of poor husbands have felt the sting of Arnolphe's raillery about their wives' infidelities, and now he—. Arnolphe interrupts to deliver a harangue on the corruptions of town, where women fool their husbands at every turn. But, Chrysalde continues, since Arnolphe has been like a demon with his relentless sarcasms about the cuckolds he found all around

40

him, he had better watch his own step now. Arnolphe tells his friend not to worry: he knows in their entirety the tricks of women, and the girl he is going to marry is all innocence. He has deliberately chosen a girl whom Chrysalde considers silly; he doesn't want a wife with an intellect. It is enough for him if his wife will be able to sew, spin, say her prayers, and love him. He would much prefer a stupid, ugly woman to a brilliant beautiful one. But how can a stupid one know what it is to be virtuous? his friend asks. Will it not, moreover, be a bore to have a stupid wife? Arnolphe pooh-poohs these reservations. He chose Agnès for his wife when she was only four. He procured her from a poor home, brought her up in a solitary little convent, and since then has kept her not in his house, but in a place where no one ever comes but the simplest sort of people. He invites Chrysalde to sup with them tonight so that he may meet Agnès and judge for himself. She is indeed so pure that the other day she asked her guardian whether children were born through the ears.

Chrysalde cannot understand why at the age of forty-two Arnolphe has changed his name to de la Souche; Arnolphe did not like his name, however, because Arnulphus in the middle ages was the patron saint of deceived husbands.

Arnolphe knocks at a door of the house where he is keeping Agnès and, after some difficulty, is admitted by his servants, Georgette and Alain, two country simpletons. He asks after Agnès. Was she sad after he left last time? GEORGETTE: "We never heard a horse, a donkey or a mule pass without her thinking it was you."

Agnès appears. Arnolphe asks if she is glad of his return; she answers: "Heaven be thanked." She has been making him nightshirts and caps, and now is making caps for herself. He finds such occupations far superior to the literary accomplishments of women of fashion.

After she goes off, Horace comes in. He had sought
Arnolphe at his own house but found him not at home.
Arnolphe is delighted to see the youth, whom he has known
since infancy, and inquires after the boy's father, Oronte.
Oronte will be coming to town any day. They speak of
Enrique, who has returned from a fourteen years' absence in
America with a fortune.

Horace is in need of a hundred pistoles, and borrows
them from Arnolphe, who is clearly fond of the lad. How
does Horace like the town? Has he smitten any married
woman yet in this city of cuckolds? "Men with your figure
can do more than men with money. You were made to make
someone a cuckold." Horace admits that his heart has been
struck with love by a certain fair damsel; she seems to recip-
rocate his feelings. Pointing to Arnolphe's second house, he
adds that she lives there. The man who is her guardian is a
fool in trying to keep her hidden. Her name is Agnès. Does
Arnolphe know her guardian? Yes. Isn't he a fool? Jealous?
Stupid? Horace gathers from the older man's agitation that he
agrees with the description. Well, Horace adds, the reason he
needs the money he has just borrowed is that he must use it to
consummate his love for Agnès. He asks Arnolphe to keep his
secret, and leaves. Alone, Arnolphe is in a state of misery.

ACT II. He has tried to find Horace again to learn more,
but has failed. He is determined to foil the young man's plans.
He knocks at the door, and the two servants come out. He
wishes to question them but is so choked with wrath that he
can hardly speak. He wants to know how Horace was ever
admitted into the house, but his manner is so terrifying that
Alain and Georgette almost faint in terror. Perhaps it will be
better to learn the truth from Agnès. He goes into the house
and asks the two servants to wait for him. Alain and Georgette

in their simple-minded style discuss Arnolphe's jealousy, which they cannot quite understand.

Arnolphe brings Agnès out, and dismisses the servants. He tries to wind his way into the subject, and begins with talk about the weather. HE: "Any news?" SHE: "The kitten is dead." HE: "What did you do these past nine or ten days?" SHE: "Six shirts, I believe, and six nightcaps too." Some neighbors, he says, have told him that an unknown youth has been in the house and talked with her; he was willing to bet them that they were lying. SHE: "Oh, Heavens, don't bet. You'll surely lose." Why, the young man was hardly ever out of the house. (Well, thinks Arnolphe, at least her honest confession proves her purity.) I thought, says Arnolphe, I forbade you to see anyone. Oh, she replies, if you knew the facts, you would have done the same. She was working in the open air on the balcony, when a handsome young man passed by below. He bowed, she bowed in return. Thus, they exchanged three salutations silently. He went by, came back, went by again, each time bowing. She returned each bow. If night had not fallen there would have been no end to this display of good manners. The next day an old woman appeared at the door to tell her that she had wounded someone's heart. It was the young man she had seen from the balcony. Her eyes had done it. The poor fellow was pining away. What could she do? she asked the old woman. The answer: if you don't allow him to see and speak with you, he'll be in his grave within three days. Agnès concludes: "And that is how he came to see me and got cured." Could she, who cannot see a chicken die without weeping, have done less to atone for her unintended cruelty?

"All this comes only from an innocent heart," Arnolphe muses; it is his fault for having been absent. He tries to smother his rage, and asks her how the youth conducted himself. Oh, the young man was delighted to see her, gave her a lovely casket, and large tips to the servants. He swore he loved Agnès with unparalleled passion, and spoke with the rarest charm and sweetness. Did he bestow any caresses on her? Oh, many; he never tired of kissing her hands and arms. Did he take anything from her? Arnolphe's manner terrifies her, when she answers in the affirmative, and it is some time before she has the courage to tell him—yes, the youth took the ribbon Arnolphe gave her. Half-relieved, Arnolphe asks: "To cure the illness which he said had seized him, didn't he ask for any other remedy?" SHE: "No. But you can guess that I would have granted anything that might have done him good, if he had asked for it."

Arnolphe thanks his stars for her innocence. He will never leave her alone again. He warns her that her gallant wished only to deceive her; it is a sin to let a man kiss her hands and warm her heart. How can that be? she asks—it is all so agreeable! The sin is taken away only by marriage, he tells her. "Then marry me at once," she cries. He has come back to town to do just that. She is delighted: he will make her so happy! ARNOLPHE: "To see you happy is my desire." AGNÈS: "How much I am obliged to you, and what satisfaction I shall have with him." Alas! she has misunderstood. With *him* (Horace) she is to break off all communication at once; if he comes again she is to shut the door in his face, and throw a stone at him if he is passing. Agnès is overwhelmed with confusion at these unexpected commands.

ACT III. Arnolphe congratulates Agnès in having been saved from perdition in the nick of time by his care of her. Georgette and Alain swear that Horace will never get in the house again.

Arnolphe tells Agnès that it is himself whom he has selected as her bridegroom. "You ought to thank your stars a

hundred times a day when you remember your former low
condition and also to marvel at my kindness in raising you
from a poor country girl to the rank of the wife of a citizen;
and to enjoy the bed and the embraces of a man . . . whose
heart has refused a score of women the honor he will confer
upon you." She must never forget how insignificant she would
be without this marriage. She must also remember that the
husband is supreme and omnipotent; a wife owes her spouse
all "docility, obedience, meekness, and profound respect," for
he is her lord and master. If she ever stains her honor, she will
boil in Hell for eternity. He gives her a little book containing
maxims on the duties of a wife: the wife must bedeck herself no more than her husband wishes, must not use cosmetics,
must look neither to left nor right in public, must see only
those her husband invites, must refuse gifts from men, must
not own pen and ink, must avoid social gatherings and
gambling, etc. Arnolphe remembers he has a brief engage-
ment, and asks her to go into the house. Alone, he feels sure
that he can mould her into the kind of wife he wishes to
have, just because she is simple.

Horace comes in, having again sought Arnolphe at his
other house. How is Horace's love-affair going? Alas, cruel
fate has brought back the girl's guardian; worse luck, the
guardian has discovered what has passed in private between
the two lovers. How so, in so brief a time? All Horace knows
is that he tried to visit her again, but this time the servants
shut the door in his face. Agnès, moreover, threw a stone at
him from the balcony. Arnolphe pretends sympathy. But what
astonishes Horace is another aspect of the incident. Love is a
great tutor, and has taught Agnès rapidly, for all her simplicity.
When she threw the stone, she called out to him: "I know
all you'd say, and *there*'s my answer." Attached to the stone
was a letter. Horace reads the letter. In it Agnès says that she

begins to suspect that she has been kept deliberately in ignorance; she has been assured that all young men are de-
ceivers, but she cannot believe this of Horace; let him tell her
frankly whether he has been talking truth to her. Arnolphe
gasps with suppressed anguish at all this. Horace asks for his
help, but Arnolphe begs out, saying he has a pressing engage-
ment, and the youth leaves. Arnolphe soliloquizes on his
misery, his misplaced trust in Agnès, his jealousy. What is he
to do? He loves her to distraction.

ACT IV.   Alone, Arnolphe declares that there is no peace
of mind for him. Agnès is not the least bit upset at what she
has done. The more composed she looked, the nearer he felt to
death—yet she never looked lovelier. The Notary appears, but
Arnolphe is too agitated to speak with him about the marriage, and walks off. The Notary thinks him mad.

Arnolphe again instructs the servants concerning Horace,
and rehearses with them what they are to do and say in the
way of insult if the youth appears. He is satisfied that they will
make good watch-dogs now. Arnolphe also decides to get the
cobbler on the corner to play the spy for him.

Horace comes in again, happy to see his old friend. Just
now, Agnès gave him a sign from the balcony, came down into
the garden, and opened the door. They were scarcely in her
room when they heard her guardian, and she was forced to
lock her lover in the wardrobe. Horace did not see him, but
heard him pacing up and down in great agitation silently, but
kicking at everything in sight, and breaking the vases on the
mantel. Eventually the guardian quitted the room without
saying what was bothering him. Horace quickly made his
exit, but is to come back to her room tonight; he is to emit
three hems, and then ascend by a ladder. He is off to make

the preparations for his bliss. Arnolphe soliloquizes on the evil destiny which allows him no time to breathe. Must he, a mature man, be the dupe of a simple girl and scatterbrained boy? He had thought to avoid the common fate of husbands, and finds himself threatened with the same disgrace. At any rate, he can prevent the carrying out of the plans of the two young people.

Chrysalde arrives, as invited, for the supper, only to find that the feast is called off. He lectures Arnolphe on making too much fuss about the cuckolding to which his friend insists all husbands are subject. Chrysalde, for one, would prefer to be married to a wife who does him some trifling wrong than to a dragon of virtue, one of these she-devils of respectability. If a man is fated to be cuckolded, let him bear it with some patience. Arnolphe explodes at his advice: he will find a remedy against any such possibility. Chrysalde leaves, and Arnolphe warns his servants that Horace proposes using a ladder tonight; he wants them to be armed with cudgels with which to belabor Horace, when he has climbed to the last round of the ladder.

ACT V. Arnolphe upbraids his servants: he told them to cudgel Horace, not to murder him. What will Horace's father say when he finds his son is dead?

Enter Horace, very much alive. Just as he was reaching Agnès' window, he beheld two persons—raising their arms against him. He missed his footing and fell to the ground; a little bruise spared him heavy blows. Since he lay quiet for a while his assailants must have taken him for dead, for they raised a great cry, accusing each other, and came in the dark to feel if he were dead. He behaved like a corpse, and they ran away terrified. Agnès, having heard them, was soon

bending over him and found him unhurt. She now refused
to return to her room and confided her innocence to Horace's
honor. He would rather die than wrong her; and nothing but
death shall part them. He asks if Arnolphe will take care of
her for a while (in his other house, the only house in town
that Horace knows he has)—for a day or two, anyway.
Arnolphe agrees. But it is almost daybreak, and if Horace
wishes her whereabouts to remain secret, Horace had better
bring her to the dark alley of Arnolphe's (other) house.
Arnolphe quickly muffles himself up in his cloak.

Horace brings Agnès in and hands her over to the muffled
Arnolphe, and promises to join her soon. He goes out.
Arnolphe alters his voice to say that he has a room where she
will be safe enough. Then he opens his cloak and reveals himself. "So, so. Young as you are, you can still play such pranks!"
Where did she learn to be such a deceiver, despite all his kindness? "Little viper that I have warmed in bosom!" he cries.
She protests that she does not know why he scolds her. She is
but following his teaching that she ought to marry to avoid
sin. "I meant you to be my wife myself!" "But he is more to
my liking as a husband. . . . He makes it sound so full of joy
that I long to marry him." "Traitress! That's because you love
him!" "Yes, I love him!" "Don't you love me?" "Alas, no!"
"Why don't you love me, Madame Impertinence?" "Why
didn't you make me love you, as he did?" She denies that she
owes as much to Arnolphe as she does to Horace, and is quite
saucy with him. Arnolphe feels he ought to cuff her, but his
love for her prevents that. He tries to talk her into rejecting
Horace, and promises to buy her beautiful clothes and to
fondle her day and night. What proof does she want of his
love? Would she have him weep, beat himself, tear out his
hair, kill himself? He will, if she wishes. She bids him stop;
none of this touches her; "Horace can do more with a couple

of words." Her cruelty turns Arnolphe's thoughts to sending her to a convent. He confides her to the watch of Alain.

Horace comes in, overwhelmed with worry. His father has just arrived with Enrique, to whose daughter Horace is destined to be married. Will not Arnolphe try to dissuade his friend from forcing Horace into such a union? Oronte (Horace's father) and Enrique come in with Chrysalde, as Horace and Arnolphe retire to the back of the stage. The newcomers discuss Horace's betrothal to Enrique's daughter. Arnolphe comes forward and embraces his old friend Oronte. He warns Oronte that Horace's heart is pledged elsewhere but counsels that his old friend exert his parental authority and insist on the marriage as earlier planned. Chrysalde is against such coercion; he also corrects Oronte when he addresses Arnolphe by his former name: Agnès' guardian is now Monsieur de la Souche. Already angered by Arnolphe's treachery, Horace now hears this name associated for the first time with Arnolphe. Now Horace knows who he is. Since Agnès is ready to throw herself from the window, Georgette takes her out. She appeals to Horace, who is overwhelmed in sorrow. The others do not understand what is happening, and Arnolphe urges Oronte to hasten the planned marriage of his son. Oronte asks: but doesn't Arnolphe know that Enrique's daughter is living in Arnolphe's (second) house? Her parents' marriage was secret, and when the child was born she was put out to nurse under an assumed name. Enrique had to leave the country, and on his return now to France with the fortune he has made, he at once sought out his daughter's nurse; the country-woman told him that she had handed the child over at the age of four to Arnolphe. Chrysalde whispers to his friend that fortune has been kind to him; by not marrying he will escape the destiny of becoming a cuckold. Full of rage Arnolphe runs off. Agnès is reunited to her father and pledged to Horace. Chrysalde suggests that they go within and try to console poor Arnolphe.

◆ Molière himself enacted the role of Arnolphe. One wonders at his thoughts during the performances. Whatever the personal element, it was in this play that Molière for the first time demonstrated his genius for being quite serious in the midst of bubbling comedy. Its clear statement of the right of young people to choose their own loved ones and of the fact that the dictates of nature cannot be suppressed by authority is an early sign of Molière's undeviating loyalty to truth and common sense.

But the play won a great many enemies, and was even accused of indecency. Molière decided to answer his critics in *The School for Wives Criticized* (June 1, 1663), a prose piece in one act. Although less a play than a spirited dialogue, it was very popular and frequently presented along with *The School for Wives*. The Marquis represents the noble patron who is ready to judge a work without having seen or read it; Lysidas is the envious pedant; Climène (an early study for Philaminte of *The Learned Ladies*) is the lady "whose ears are chaster than the rest of her anatomy." Molière's idea of using this self-critical technique was later adopted by other writers.

THE SCHOOL FOR
WIVES CRITICIZED

La Critique de L'École des femmes

SCENE: *Paris in the house of Uranie*

Persons of the Drama

Uranie
Élise
Climène
The Marquis
Galopin: *a lackey*
Dorante: *a knight*
Lysidas: *a poet*

Élise asks Uranie to rid her of the troublesome Marquis with his unending quips. Galopin a lackey comes in to announce Climène. Tell her I'm not in, says Uranie. It's too late, the lackey has already said otherwise. Though a woman of rank, says Élise, Climène is very stupid, and her affectations are beyond enduring. Climène enters exhausted, and calls immediately for a chair. She has been near fainting ever since she left Molière's theatre at the Palais Royal. She has just seen the villainous *The School for Wives,* and will be ill a fortnight Uranie and Élise have heard the play without ill effects; the play, says Uranie, should be more medicinal than sickness provoking. Climène cries that certain common phrases (such as "children through the ear") made her stomach turn; no gentlewoman could see that play without confusion because of the improprieties in it. Uranie declares she herself could not find any, and asks for a sample passage. Well, for instance, the scene (Act II) in which Agnès tells what Horace took from her. What was indecent about that? Well, snorts Climène, if Uranie doesn't see that, there's no use of talking. Uranie lectures her on false modesty and on women whose ears are chaster than all the rest of their anatomy. Climène insists that the passage in question was full of obscene suggestion. Élise, the little hypocrite, flatters Climène and mockingly pretends to agree with her.

The Marquis comes in. He has just come from Molière's play too, and found it silly, wretched, and, worst of all, the crowd at the theatre was insufferably large. Dorante enters and says that he has heard the play condemned for the very things for which others praise it. The Marquis thinks the comedy detestable; Dorante thinks the Marquis' judgment detestable. Dorante wishes to hear the Marquis' reasons; why is the comedy detestable? "It is detestable—because it is detestable." What are its faults? "I didn't take the trouble to listen to it . . . You had only to hear the continual outbursts of laughter from the pit." It's enough to prove the work's utter worthlessness, when people of no rank approve of it. Dorante dislikes this snobbery: the other day, a nobleman who was sitting on the stage got gloomier the more the pit was laughing, and thus provided a second comedy. Good taste and judgment, Dorante continues, bear no relationship to the location of the spectator in a theatre. The Marquis scorns Dorante as a defender of the pit, but the latter has no patience with noblemen who judge without knowledge. The Marquis counters with the fact that Lysander, their friend, detests Molière's play too. The trouble with Lysander, says Dorante, is that he simply must be the first in everything; he cannot bear to have anyone else praise a thing before he does; when that happens he is against the work. And the Marchioness Araminte, who declares *The School for Wives* indecent? Oh, that lady has a positive genius for finding indecencies where there aren't any, in order to pass as a woman of enormous virtue.

Lysidas, the author, comes in. He at first feigns that as a writer himself he must speak cautiously of another's work. Pressed, he says the play is fine—but his tone causes the rest to know he means otherwise. Urged to go on, he declares that there can be no comparison between these trifling comedies and serious works. Uranie defends comedies: they are as difficult to write well as tragedies. Dorante goes further: comedies are more difficult; "it is much easier to soar with grand sentiments, . . . to impeach destiny and upbraid the gods, than to broach ridicule in a fit manner, and to make the shortcomings of men agreeable on the boards." In a comedy "you must be merry, and it's hard to make the people of rank laugh." The Marquis and Climène found nothing to laugh at in *The School for Wives*. Lysidas found the wit insipid. He jeers ironically at the fact that the Court liked the play. Dorante defends the Court as the breeding-ground of taste and wit; there are a few ridiculous people at Court, to be sure, but so are there among authors too—with "their greed of praise, their emptiness of thought, . . . their cliques." Lysidas declares that

Molière's play has a hundred faults. URANIE: "It's odd the way you gentlemen-poets always abuse the plays which everyone enjoys, and praise only those no one goes to see." LYSIDAS: Any one who has read Aristotle and Horace will see that Molière breaks all the rules. DORANTE: Anyone hearing you talk would think the rules were mysterious; they are simply the dictates of good sense; isn't the rule of all rules to please? Lysidas commences to castigate the play for breaking all the laws of dramatic composition, even if it does please Dorante. LYSIDAS: Moreover, doesn't Arnolphe give Horace the money too easily? aren't the maxims offensive to religion? isn't Arnolphe too ridiculous in the last act in the expression of his love for Agnès? The Marquis, Climène and Élise enthusiastically second all of Lysidas' criticism. Uranie is of the conviction that the power of the play consists in just this: that a sensible man who is warned of everything cannot nonetheless escape his fate. Dorante defends the play against the other objections raised, but the Marquis, now bored, begins humming to end the discussion. Uranie thinks a little comedy might be made out of the things they themselves have been saying, and Dorante is asked to write it all out and hand it to Molière. Supper is announced, and thus the piece ends.

◆ It is worthy of note that Élise was the first part taken by Molière's wife. Thereafter he wrote for her roles calling for coquetry and a sharp wit, as in the case of Célimène in *The Misanthrope*. Perhaps the most noteworthy passage in this piece is his defence of comedy: "When you paint men, you must paint them after nature. We look for the recognizable in these portraits; you have accomplished nothing if you cannot make us recognize the people of our time." This is a perfect statement of Molière's own accomplishment.

THE IMPROMPTU AT VERSAILLES

The School for Wives Criticized made fresh enemies for Molière among people of fashion. Thirsting for revenge because of his barbs at them, they hired a young unknown, Boursault (1638-1701), a man of limited talents though of open nature, to write for the rival company at the Hôtel de Bourgogne a comedy in which *The School for Wives* should be ridiculed. This piece was entitled *The Painter's Portrait.* It is said that the King sent for Molière to Versailles and commanded his favorite comic dramatic to reply to his critics, and granted the Court theatre for his use. Molière had only a few days, but the challenge was great. The result was the sparkling one-act prose comedy, *The Impromptu at Versailles,* which was performed on October 14, 1663, and later at Paris with great success. It seems to have silenced the opposition for the moment.

When the curtain was opened it must have been something of a shock for the audience to see Molière and his troupe in their everyday apparel and in their own persons, getting ready a rehearsal, as though no audience were present.

THE IMPROMPTU
AT VERSAILLES

L'Impromptu de Versailles

Persons of the Drama

Molière: *a foolish marquis*
Brécourt: *a man of rank*
De la Grange: *a foolish marquis*
Du Croisy: *a poet*
La Thorillière: *a boring marquis*
Béjart: *a man who takes care of everything*
Mlle. Du Parc: *a marchioness*
Mlle. Béjart: *a prude*
Mlle. De Brie: *a wise coquette*
Mlle. Molière: *a satirical wit*
Mlle. Du Croisy: *a whining gipsy*
Mlle. Hervé: *a precious chambermaid*

Molière is calling to his fellow-actors offstage. He is beside himself with anxiety, and they are driving him to distraction, as they leisurely appear one by one. Since the King won't be coming for several hours, let us rehearse, Molière says. The actors are in a state: they haven't had time to learn their parts, and would prefer to have nothing to do with the performance. None of them feels sorry for *him;* after all, he wrote the piece. MOLIÈRE: Do they think he hasn't troubles enough having to amuse such an audience as the Court? He, too, would give anything to be out of this enterprise, but he could hardly refuse the command of the King. Let us, he pleads, get on with the rehearsal. But what are they to do if they don't know their lines? Let them fill them in out of their own heads; after all it's prose. MLLE. BÉJART: "Prose is harder than verse." MLLE. MOLIÈRE (the dramatist's wife): "You ought to write a comedy in which you're the only actor."

Molière says that he had thought of writing a comedy in which a poet offers a strolling company his play. He would ask: "Have you actors and actresses able to do justice to my play?" The poet would be reassured on that point. Who will play the King? An actor "of vast circumference, who'd fill a throne." Here Molière imitates the manner of the fat Montfleury, of the rival company at the Hôtel de Bourgogne, ranting in that actor's style. Next comes an imitation of the styles of Madeleine de Beauchâteau and her husband, of the rival troupe, in the roles of lovers. She maintains a smiling face in the midst of deepest affliction. Other members of that theatre are also mimicked.

However, Molière now turns to the business in hand. His wife objects to there being "Marquises again." MOLIÈRE: "What the devil do you expect me to invent for a character pleasing to the audience? These days the Marquis is the funny character. . . . In all our pieces there must always be a ridiculous Marquis." He distributes the parts, and points out that some of them are similar to the roles his troupe acted in *The School for Wives Criticized.*

As they are about to begin their rehearsal, La Thorillière, a fidgetty Marquis comes in, much to Molière's annoyance. The Marquis has just come from a place where he has been praising Molière. He is anxious to know all about the play they are to rehearse, how they will be dressed (MOLIÈRE: "As you see"), when the King is coming, etc. Molière is furious at this waste of time. The Marquis now starts flirting with two of the actresses. Another actress lets him know he is interfering with their rehearsal. He blandly suggests that they go right ahead with it and not mind him. Molière makes it clear that the troupe much prefers no audience during rehearsal. They finally get rid of the Marquis.

The play is to open with the meeting of two Marquises; the other actors must make room; MOLIÈRE: "for a couple of Marquises require lots of room." Molière criticizes the speech of the other Marquis as not pitched high enough to distinguish him from the vulgar. (Molière is enacting the first Marquis.)

MOLIÈRE: I don't want Molière imitating me.

LA GRANGE: Yet I do think, Marquis, that it is you he mimicks in *The School for Wives Criticized*.

MOLIÈRE: Me? Good lord! It's *you*.

LA GRANGE: Ah! Most kind of you to clothe me in your own character!

MOLIÈRE: 'S death, but you are droll, giving me what is your own!

The two Marquises bet a hundred pistoles that it was the other whom the dramatist had been ridiculing. They see Brécourt, who is supposed to act a Man of Quality (Molière has to stop him and tell him *not* to sound like a Marquis), and ask him to decide which of the two the dramatist had lampooned. Brécourt agrees with neither. He overheard Molière the other day telling some people that his satire is general, not aimed at individuals; he was sick of being told that he had this or that one in mind when writing his comedies. It is "the business of comedy to show in a general way all the shortcomings of men, especially those of our own time." The two Marquises are not satisfied, but one of them asks whether Molière has not exhausted his material. How is that possible, asks Brécourt, when we continue to provide him with plenty of subjects? Are not there always false friends who tear one another to pieces behind their backs? shameless sycophants? empty flatterers? treacherous worshippers of fortune? hangers-on of the Court? fawners upon all the world? "Molière will always have more subjects than he can use."

Climène and Élise (from *The School for Wives Criticized*) are the next to appear. There is an exchange of elaborate compliments. Lysidas has just told them that someone called Boursault has written a play against Molière. Actually, many people have contributed to this new play, and much is expected of it; "since all authors and actors regard Molière as their arch enemy," everyone has united against him. But the people of rank do not wish to claim authorship, and hence have chosen an unknown author. Molière shall be taught not to satirize everyone. The Marquises are delighted. In any case, all those who have a grudge against Molière will applaud the new play, whether it prove good or bad. "Why does he write those wicked plays of his which all Paris goes to see, and in which he depicts people so well that everyone recognizes himself in them?" Why doesn't he write like Lysidas? It's true no one would come to see plays like them, but no one would be against the author. They are all going to see *The Painter's Portrait* by Boursault. Molière will have to hide his head. Not at all, counters Brécourt; Molière intends to take a seat on the stage and laugh with the rest. [Molière actually did this.] The actors say that they expect some kind of reply from the attacked dramatist. BRÉCOURT: "I'd think him a great fool if he took the trouble to answer their invectives"; the best thing Molière can do is write a new play to take their audiences away from them.

Molière now speaks in his own person. To the suggestion that he attack Boursault he says: "A fine subject for amusement Boursault would be! . . . How could he be made to appear entertaining? . . . He's a man with nothing to lose . . . I don't intend any reply. . . . Let them cry all the evil they wish of my plays. . . . Let them take our leavings . . . and bring them on their own stage . . . I gladly grant them my works, my figure, my attitudes, my words, my voice, my style of acting, to make what they will of them, if they can grasp any profit from that." All I ask is that they leave my private life and my family's alone, Molière continues. . . . But let's get on with the rehearsal.

Béjart comes in to say that the King has arrived and is waiting for them to begin the performance. Molière tries to brace his company's desperate spirits. A procession of busybodies comes in, one after the other, urging the troupe to start proceedings. Béjart re-enters with good news; the King, hearing of their production troubles, defers the comedy to some later date. He will be content with whatever work they have ready for presentation.

THE FORCED MARRIAGE

The King next asked Molière for a comedy in the style of *The Bores,* that is, a comedy (combined with ballet) which should employ the courtiers themselves. Having just received a pension of a thousand livres, Molière was more than anxious to oblige. On January 29, 1664, in the salon of the Queen

Mother at the Louvre, *The Forced Marriage* (*Le Mariage forcé*), originally a prose work in three acts but later reduced to a one-act comedy-ballet, was first performed. The King appeared as one of the gypsies in the play. Sganarelle is seen here again, in a plot taken from Rabelais. Of all of Molière's court-pieces, this is the finest. The comedy proceeds from the disparity between the years of the aged gallant and the young coquette he loves; he is forced into a marriage with the full surety that the fate of a cuckold awaits him. The aged Sganarelle wishes to marry the young and pretty coquette, Dorimène, who, for her own part, is anxious to escape from her parents' protection. The old fellow consults the opinion of his neighbor Géronimo, of the Aristotelian philosopher Pancrace, of the rival philosopher Marphurius, and finally of two gypsies who reply only with smiles, songs, and dance. Brought to his senses by the foolhardy talk of Dorimène, Sganarelle breaks with her. But she has a brother, the bully Alcidas, who forces Sganarelle to make good his word, much to the delight of her father, who praises God that he is rid of her.

THE PRINCESS OF ELIS

In May, 1664, the King entertained the Queen-mother and Queen Maria Theresa with an extravagant series of entertainments as Versailles. During the festivities Molière's five-act comedy-ballet, partly in verse, partly in prose, *The Princess of Elis* (*La Princesse d'Élide*) was presented, its subject the male versus the female in love. Composed at the request of the King, the work is romantic in tone, but the dramatist seems under too much constraint here: it is one of his weakest works. The haste in which he had to compose it did nothing to encourage him to be at his best.

TARTUFFE

In honor of his mistress, Mlle. de la Vallière, Louis XIV now arranged another festival at Versailles. For the occasion Molière presented on May 8, 1664, the masterpiece, *Tartuffe,* then a work in three acts. (It has never been settled whether those three acts were a complete play or the opening three acts of an unfinished play, which when completed was the five-act verse comedy we now know.) The King found it a very diverting piece. But Molière's enemies had summoned their powers. When the piece was repeated four days later with success, the Archbishop of Paris, Hardouin de Péréfixe, hastened to inform the King that *Tartuffe* might have some serious "bad effects." Anne of Austria added her voice to the rising storm, the King allowed himself to be influenced, and the play was forbidden further performance because it might jeopardize religion. Presently, during the King's sojourn at Fontainebleau, the curé of St. Barthélemy, Roullé, published a libelous and violent work congratulating Louis for having forbidden a play, ready for public presentation, which Molière, "a devil clothed in human flesh and attired like a man" had "brought forth from his diabolical mind." His enemies grew the stronger—who abused him, most absurdly, with the charge of attacking piety in general and the Jesuits in particular. Nothing is clearer than that the dramatist was aiming his shafts only at religious hypocrites.

DON JUAN

The interdiction of *Tartuffe* upset Molière's theatrical plans. *The Misanthrope,* on which he had been working, was not ready yet. He, therefore, composed *Don Juan,* on a subject which was stylish; he felt certain of success. It was seen at the Palais Royal on February 15, 1665. But this play was also an attack on hypocrites, and his enemies only increased their fury. After some fifteen performances the censor authorized the stopping of this work. Actually, the attack on hypocrisy is graver in this play than in *Tartuffe;* it bears a unique place among Molière's masterpieces, and is closest of all his works to the Shakespearean conception of comedy in its admixture of the tragic with the comic. The French consider the complexity of its hero somewhat puzzling; it is a role which has been the ambition of leading French actors to perform, but it is also held to be tremendously difficult.

The story comes from Spain. An old legend tells how Don Juan de Tenorio, Governor of Seville, eloped with the daughter of the Commander Gonzalo, whom he killed in a duel, and who, after his burial, had a fine statue erected to him. Don Juan, who made the utmost of the privileges of his rank, insulted the Commander's statue. It came down from its marble tomb, seized the impious murderer, and hurled him into the depths of Hell.

The Spanish dramatist Tirso de Molina (pen-name for the monk Gabriel Tellez) wrote a comedy on the legend called *The Seducer of Seville and the Stone Guest.* Its story tells of how Don Juan, having seduced the Duchess Isabella at Naples, is ordered seized by the King. Don Juan escapes and is shipwrecked on the coast of Spain at Tarragona. There he seduces a fisherman's daughter with the promise of marriage; she, abandoned, drowns herself. Next, at Seville, disguised as his friend the Marquis de la Mota, Don Juan repeats his conduct with the Commander's daughter, Donna Anna. He kills the Commander, and flees into the country.

He meets and seduces Aminta, whom also he has promised to marry. Secretly the seducer returns to Seville, and reads the inscription on the Commander's tomb, which says that the buried father waits "until God shall avenge him on a traitor." Don Juan insults the statue and invites it to dine with him. The statue appears and asks Don Juan to feast with him the next night in the chapel. He accepts. The two dine on vipers, scorpions, and vinegar. Don Juan repents of his misdeeds and asks for a priest to whom he may confess. In the last scene, the King at Seville repairs the sins of Don Juan by bestowing all the living women the latter has seduced in marriage upon various husbands. In Molina's play Don Juan is neither atheistic nor a professional seducer: he is rather an easy-going, self-indulgent man who keeps postponing the day of repentence. His basic belief in the Church is never questioned, and at the end he is received again into it.

In his five-act prose comedy Molière's atheist hero has been much altered, and moreover bears little resemblance to the gallery of leading characters in the dramatist's other plays. His Don Juan is witty and elegant, to be sure, but unpleasant. This young, wealthy, powerful, well-mannered nobleman is not ridiculous but terrifying. After all his misdeeds, he takes on the most digusting of all vices, hypocrisy. This hero seems less interested in satisfying his lecherous passions than in deliberately outraging human decency; by preference it is innocence and goodness which he chooses to corrupt. His elegance makes him all the more horrifying.

At the first performance the scene between him and the poor man, many of the sallies exchanged between him and Sganarelle, and some other passages gave rise to so much objection that they had to be deleted at once. The role of Sganarelle, by this time an old friend to Molière's audiences and here a servant to Don Juan, was performed by Molière.

One of the greatest of all operas, Mozart's *Don Giovanni*, has a libretto on this story, but it seems rather closer to Molina than to Molière.

DON JUAN

or

THE FEAST WITH THE STONE

Don Juan, ou Le Festin de pierre

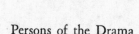

Persons of the Drama

Don Juan: *Don Louis' son*
Sganarelle: *Don Juan's valet*
Elvire: *Don Juan's wife*
Gusman: *Elvire's squire*
Don Carlos ⎫
Don Alonse ⎭ *Elvire's brothers*
Don Louis: *Don Juan's father*
Francisque: *a poor man*
Charlotte ⎫
Mathurine ⎭ *peasants*
Pierrot: *a peasant*
The Statue of the Commandant
La Violette ⎫
Ragotin ⎭ *Don Juan's lackeys*
Monsieur Dimanche: *a tradesman*
La Ramée: *a ruffian*

66

Attendants of Don Juan
Attendants of Don Carlos and Don Alonse
A Ghost

ACT I. A palace. Sganarelle, snuff-box in hand, is singing to Donna Elvire's gentleman-usher, Gusman, the praises
of tobacco. Donna Elvire, Don Juan's wife, having learned of
her husband's abrupt departure, has followed him. Sganarelle
foresees it will do her little good. Gusman cannot understand
how after all the violence of Don Juan's courtship—which
went as far as carrying her off from a convent—he can now
betray his wife. SGANARELLE: If you knew him, you'd see it's
easy enough for him; Don Juan is one of the world's greatest
scoundrels, an atheist, half-madman, a demon, who lives like
a brute. "Marriage means nothing to him: it's his usual method
of entrapping women. He marries them whenever he can . . .
If I were to give you the list of his wives . . . it would take all
night . . . I'd rather serve the Devil than him, he's made me
witness so many horrors. . . . When a nobleman is wicked, it
is terrible." Sganarelle serves him out of fear. Let Gusman
respect Sganarelle's confidences; if they are repeated, he will
flatly deny them. Gusman goes out as Don Juan enters.

Sganarelle tells his master that Gusman is much upset
about their abandoning of Donna Elvire. Don Juan asks his
servant for his own explanation; Sganarelle guesses a new
love affair—and, if he may speak frankly, he thinks it very
wrong to be making love on all sides. DON JUAN: Should a
man renounce the world for just one woman? All beautiful
women have the right to men's love. The fact that one loves
a woman should not make him unjust to the rest of the sex.
"The entire pleasure in love lies in the fact that it won't last."
It is a great joy, too, to watch a woman capitulate a degree
at a time as one lays siege to her. "Once one succeeds, there's

nothing left. . . . Like Alexander I still wish for new worlds
to conquer." Sganarelle answers that his master's eloquence
has muddled him and routed all his arguments, but cautiously
he warns him against trifling with the holy sacrament of marriage. Don Juan tells him he doesn't like being preached at.
But in a roundabout way Sganarelle continues: how dare
one set oneself up against Heaven? does any nobleman think
that because he's dressed in the height of fashion that that
makes him any the wiser? (Sganarelle describes the clothes
Don Juan is wearing without stating that he means his master.) The evil-liver is bound to come to a bad end. His master
tells him to shut up; all he can think of is his new love.
Doesn't Don Juan tremble when he remembers how he killed
the Commander only six months ago? "Why should I fear?
Didn't I kill him properly?" "Very properly! He can't complain."

Don Juan prefers to talk of his present obsession. She
has just arrived with a man she is going to marry. He met
them a few days ago, and never saw a couple more in love. He
immediately became jealous of their happiness, and thought
how fine it would be to break up their mutual devotion. Today
the husband-to-be is going sailing; Don Juan has engaged
some men and a boat to abduct her so he can gratify his
passion.

Donna Elvire enters, and the Don confesses surprise at
seeing her in this place. His behavior convinces her that all
the excuses she has tried to make for him are without basis.
Let him tell her directly the reasons for his departure. He
tells her to ask Sganarelle. The servant tries to beg off, but
both master and mistress insist that he speak. SGANARELLE:
"We departed because of Alexander and his other worlds."
ELVIRE: How does her husband explain this? What lies can
he frame? Don Juan answers coldly that not being a liar he

will not pretend that he loves to be with her as he once did; indeed, he left to escape from her—on grounds of conscience. It would be a sin to live with her longer, since he carried her off from a convent and made her break her vows to Heaven. He now repents of their ill-advised marriage and fears the wrath of Heaven. Elvire sees him in his true light at last, regrets having exposed herself this way, and is sure that Heaven will avenge her. Sganarelle mumurs on the wickedness of his master.

ACT II. The seashore. Charlotte and Pierrot, country-folk who speak a provincial dialect [this was something new for Moliére's theatre], are discussing a great storm at sea this morning. He and a friend saw two men struggling in the water, got into a boat, rescued them on the point of drowning, and carried them home to dry off. Two more of the company, who had saved themselves, joined the two others; one of them made sheep's eyes at Mathurine, a peasant woman. One of the men who was nearly drowned, the master of the others, "has gold all over his clothes." When the four dressed themselves Pierrot was astounded at the complication of that operation.

Pierrot tells Charlotte that he is in love with her, as she knows; they ought to get married. The only trouble is, he adds, that she doesn't love him. She protests she does. He shakes his head; the proof is otherwise; she never teases him or plays practical jokes on him as a girl who loves should. She answers: "I love you as well as I can. If you're not satis-fied, find somebody else." Perhaps, she adds, what he wants "will come all of a sudden, without planning." Seeing Don Juan and Sganarelle approach, he goes out. Charlotte moves to the back of the stage.

The Don's plot has failed because their boat overturned.

But the country-wench Mathurine, whom he has just seen can make up for it; he won't have to sigh in vain long for her. Sganarelle is amazed that instead of thanking Heaven for their rescue, his master is up to new mischief. The Don now sees the other country-girl, Charlotte. He questions her, praises her beauty, examines her teeth, declares them love-inspiring. She is too shy to say much beyond the fact that she is to marry Pierrot, the man who saved his life. DON JUAN: "Should a creature like you become the wife of a peasant?" That would be a sacrilege to her beauty. The Don tells her he loves her, will take her away and give her the position in the world she merits. Let not his suddenness alarm her: she has made him fall more deeply in love in fifteen minutes than any other could in six months. Charlotte does not know what to think; she enjoys hearing him talk, but she also knows that men from the Court only wish to lead girls astray. He assures her that he is talking of marriage, and calls Sganarelle to back up his intention. At last convinced, she allows him to kiss her hand. Pierrot comes in and interposes. The Don gives him a box on the ear. Charlotte announces that the Don is going to marry her. PIERROT: "But you're engaged to me." CHARLOTTE: "What of it? If you love me you should be glad I'm to be made a lady." When she has been raised in station, she'll do something for Pierrot: he can sell them his butter and cheese. Pierrot wishes that instead of saving Don Juan, he had given him a good rap on the head with an oar. The Don wishes to beat Pierrot for his insolence; Sganarelle intercedes and receives the blow instead. Pierrot runs off to tell Charlotte's aunt.

Mathurine comes in. She asks, "Is he courting Charlotte too?" No, it is Charlotte who is vainly courting him. He tells the same tale in Charlotte's ear. The two girls begin to

quarrel. MATHURINE: "The Gentleman saw me first." CHAR-
LOTTE: "He saw me second, and it's me he's promised to
marry." They approach him to settle the matter. He is evasive: why should he repeat what he has already said to each?
When he marries, they will know which of the two has his
heart. Again he whispers confidence into the ear of each girl,
and then exits. Sganarelle urges the girls to believe none of
the Don's tales.

Don Juan re-enters and keeps in the background. Sganarelle is speaking of his master as a knave, but seeing him
alters his tune. La Ramée, a swashbuckler, comes in and
warns the Don that he is in danger: twelve men on horseback
are looking for him. The Don makes his excuses to the girls:
they will hear from him before tomorrow night. To Sganarelle
he announces that they will both exchange clothes, so he can
escape his present danger. Sganarelle doesn't want to be killed
for his master. DON JUAN: "Happy is the servant who has the
glory of dying for his master."

ACT III. A forest. Don Juan is dressed as a country
gentleman and Sganarelle as a physician, a proposal originat-
ing with Sganarelle in lieu of the Don's first idea for a disguise. Five or six people have already consulted Sganarelle
on their diseases. He prescribed for them at random. DON
JUAN: "Why shouldn't you have the same rights as other
doctors? They've no more to do with their patients' recovery
than you." If the Don doesn't believe in medicine, at least
he must believe in Heaven? No. The Devil and Hell? No.
A life in the hereafter? That only makes the Don roar with
laughter. Sganarelle himself is a believer, despite his lack of
education. Who created the trees, rocks, earth and sky? They
didn't make themselves any more than did the Don make

himself. Doesn't the Don realize how marvelous are the operations of the mind and soul? The Don becomes impatient with all this.

A poor man enters. He directs them toward the town, and asks for a little tip; he will pray to Heaven for the Don's prosperity. THE DON: "Pray rather to Heaven to give you a coat." The poor man tells them that he prays for all who give him a coin. The Don asks, Isn't he pretty well off then? No, he is very poor. Well, then, says Don Juan, I'm going to give you a piece of gold if you'll swear a blaspheming oath here and now. The poor man is shocked, and refuses. Don Juan presses him, and even Sganarelle, pitying his extreme poverty, begs him to swear just a little. The poor man says he would rather die of hunger first. [The passages summarized in the preceding two paragraphs contain the lines Molière was compelled immediately to suppress.] The Don throws the man a coin just the same, and seeing one man being attacked by three in the forest, he runs to the rescue.

Don Juan soon returns with Don Carlos, whom he has rescued from robbers. The latter has become lost from his brother (Don Alonse) and their retinue, and would have been killed by the highwaymen had it not been for Don Juan's valor. He and his brother have been roaming about because of a sad affair in their lives. Pressed to recount it, he relates that they are searching for Don Juan Tenorio, who abducted their sister from a convent; he has been unable to catch up with him. He never saw the man. Don Juan interrupts: "He's a friend of mine and it would be low of me to allow anyone to speak ill of him." Since Don Juan has saved Don Carlos' life, he will remain silent; yet surely, no one can condone that abduction. Don Juan says that though he is the man's friend, he promises that the Don will give Don Carlos satisfaction: let the latter merely fix the time and place.

Don Alonse comes in, happy to have found his brother. Then noting Don Juan: "What, brother! Talking with our mortal enemy?" Don Juan now reveals himself to Don Carlos. Don Alonse draws his sword, but he is stayed by his brother, who speaks of his indebtedness to Don Juan, but Don Alonse says that honor has claims prior to that of gratitude. Don Carlos insists on repaying Don Juan by postponing vengeance for a few days. His brother is obdurate. DON CARLOS: "Hold, I say, brother. . . . If you try to kill him, you must first wound me." Don Carlos prevails; their honor will shine the brighter that he has been able to requite Don Juan for saving his life. They go out.

Sganarelle, who has run off to hide, now comes forward again. His master is sorry that he will have to fight so gallant a man as Don Carlos. However, he is bored with Elvire, and there is not other way out.

He notes a splendid edifice among the trees. It is the tomb and statue of the Commander, Elvire's father, whom the Don has killed. They go into the tomb. Among the various statues is an elegant one of the Commander, in the dress of a Roman emperor. SGANARELLE: "I don't think he likes to see us." DON JUAN: "Ask him if he will come and sup with me." Sganarelle considers this idiotic, but is forced to utter the invitation. The statue nods its head. Terrified, Sganarelle stutters out this amazing portent. The Don refuses to believe him, and repeats the invitation himself. The statue nods again. Shaken, the Don leaves at once.

ACT IV. A room in Don Juan's palace. The Don now insists that what they saw was an optical illusion; if Sganarelle has another word to say on the subject, he will have him lashed a thousand times. Another servant, La Violette, announces the arrival of Dimanche, a tradesman. He must want money, says the Don; why didn't they tell him the master was out? Dimanche comes in, and the Don is very courteous to him, loads with compliments, asks after Mrs. Dimanche and their daughter, as well as their little dog. He concludes: "There is nothing I wouldn't do for you. . . . Come, Mr. Dimanche, will you take supper with me?" DIMANCHE: "No, sir; I must return home at once." DON JUAN: (rising immediately) "Here, quick, a candle to light Mr. Dimanche, and let him be escorted by four or five of my servants armed." He has swept poor Dimanche off his feet, and quits the scene.

DIMANCHE: (*to* SGANARELLE) "He is so polite to me and pays me so many compliments that I can't ever ask him for money . . . Sganarelle, please speak to him about my money." SGANARELLE: "Don't worry, he'll pay you as much as he pays anyone." Sganarelle manages to push Dimanche out.

Now the Don's father, Don Louis, arrives. He perceives at once that he is not welcome. He confesses being as much fed up with his son as his son is with him. He prayed fervently for a son, and that son turns out to be the plague of his life. What a discredit to his rank is Don Juan's wicked conduct! His forebears must disown him. There is no glory in rank if one is infamous. "Rank is nothing without virtue." A nobleman who leads a vile life is a monstrosity against nature. An honest son of a porter is to be more prized than a monarch's son who has led such a life as Don Juan's. Seeing his words make no impression, Don Louis leaves, threatening to forestall Heaven by visiting on his son the punishment he deserves. Don Juan calls out after his father. "Die as soon as you can. That's the best thing you could do!"

Donna Elvire is the next to be announced. She has overcome her wrath, and is here to warn him, out of love for him, that he is hastening to the edge of a precipice. She is going to retire to a nunnery, hoping to expiate her own crime. She begs him to think of his own salvation by mending his life. (Sganarelle, moved to tears, decides his master has the heart of a tiger.) With some mischief in mind, Don Juan tries to persuade her to stay overnight, but she refuses. After she is gone, Don Juan confesses that her distress and tears rekindled some small passion in him. Her words, Sganarelle realizes, left no impression. The Don says to his servant that after another thirty years of this life, he'll think of reforming.

Supper is brought in by the other servants. There is a knocking at the door. Sganarelle goes to see who it is, and returns frightened. In answer to Don Juan's question, he nods his head as the statue had done. The Don opens the door and the Statue comes in.

Undaunted, the Don calls for another chair and plate. Sganarelle has lost his appetite and would prefer not to sit, but is forced to do so. Don Juan orders drink and a song for the Commander. Suddenly the Statue speaks: "Enough, Don Juan. I invite you to come and sup with me tomorrow. Dare you?" Don Juan accepts, and the Statue exits.

ACT V. The country. Don Juan who has been a cruel debauchee, now plays the hypocrite. He pretends to his father that he has vowed to reform. Don Louis is ecstatically happy. Don Juan delivers a self-flagellating speech on his past crimes. How could Heaven have put up with him so long? Why did not God strike him dead twenty times over? Since Heaven has been merciful, he will mend his ways, and begs his father's help. Shedding tears of joy, Don Louis forgives his son for everything, embraces him, and goes off to bear the glad tidings to Don Juan's mother.

Sganarelle has been taken in too, and expresses his joy at

his master's conversion. Don Juan calls him a booby, and laughs over his having deceived his father. He cannot explain a statue that can move and speak; but he has adopted this hypocritical conversion as a stratagem to procure the use of his father as a screen against all the enemies he has made. After all, hypocrisy is a very fashionable vice these days, and is privileged, for it closes the mouth of the world. The cloak of religion is a wonderful protection for the wicked; a holy look will justify every kind of villainy. Henceforth, under the pretext of his religious conversion, he will be in a position to persecute his enemies, accuse *them* of irreligion, and enlist against them the aid of stupid zealots.

Sganarelle finds it impossible to keep silence any longer. His master has now reached the top of abomination, and he tells him so. Let him beat him, let him kill him, but he will speak out. But poor Sganarelle is so indigant, that what he talks is utter rubbish.

Don Carlos comes in. Nothing would please him better than to end their feud: Don Juan has only to recognize Donna Elvire publicly as his wife. Still playing the hypocrite, Don Juan feigns that nothing would please him more; but that is against Heaven's will; he has reformed and must strip himself of all worldly vanities. DON CARLOS: Such a plan is not inconsistent with the company of a lawful wife. DON JUAN: Alas! She has resolved to retire to a nunnery. DON CARLOS: The family honor will not be satisfied with such a solution; she must be publicly acknowledged his wife. DON JUAN: Unfortunately that cannot be; a voice from Heaven told him he must no longer think of Donna Elvire. Don Carlos sees through the hypocrisy and promises Don Juan a duel. Don Juan hopes that Heaven will forbid his becoming involved in a fight. As Don Carlos goes off, Sganarelle is horrified at the way his master bandies Heaven's name about. DON JUAN:

"Pooh, pooh! Heaven's not so fussy as you think."

A Ghost in the form of a veiled woman enters. GHOST: "Don Juan has only a moment to avail himself of Heaven's mercy. If he doesn't repent at once, he is sure of damnation." Don Juan, unmoved, thinks he recognizes the voice. He attempts to lift the veil, and finds instead of a woman, Time with a scythe in its hand. As the Don attempts to strike it with his sword, the Ghost vanishes.

The Statue of the Commander enters.

STATUE: Wait, Don Juan. Yesterday you promised you would come and sup with me.

DON JUAN: Where shall we go?

STATUE: Let me have your hand.

DON JUAN: There it is.

STATUE: Don Juan, for those who persist in sin a terrible end awaits. . . .

DON JUAN: Oh Heavens! What is this I feel? Flames consume me within. I cannot bear it longer. My whole body is one flame. Oh! (*Thunderbolts are heard, flashes of lightning fall on him. The earth opens and swallows him. Flames burst from the spot where he has disappeared.*)

◆ This play never saw publication until some years after Molière's death. Two months after it was first acted there was published a pamphlet by a priest named de Rochemont, *Observations on a Comedy of Molière Entitled The Feast with the Stone;* it went quickly through several editions. It was full of bitterness against Molière, accusing him of plagiarism, sameness, and mocking religion; while the King is trying to destroy heresy, it said, Molière worships impiety. He makes people laugh in order to ruin them; his Agnès has corrupted more girls than the most licentious works ever written. The King will surely put an end to Molière's services to the Devil.

LOVE THE PHYSICIAN

Molière's next play was the three-act prose comedy, *Love the Physician* (*L'Amour Médecin*), produced in September, 1665, a strong attack on the medical profession, to which the dramatist was to return in two better plays, *Doctor in Spite of Himself* and the *Imaginary Invalid*. This work was written on short notice on the demand of the King for a new play, and its harshness may be owing to Molière's own bitterness over the fate of *Tartuffe* and *Don Juan*. In his preface the author says: "It is the most rapidly composed of all which have been commanded by his Majesty. When I say that it was sketched, written, learned and acted in five days, I speak only what is true. . . . Everybody knows that comedies are written to be performed; I counsel nobody to read this unless he have the ability to imagine the stage-business."

Molière's satire here was aimed at certain doctors whose patients were members of the world of fashion, as well as at the patients themselves. Four doctors are summoned for consultation. Instead of considering the patient's ills, they talk about everything else under the sun. In despair over his daughter's condition, Sganarelle procures medicine from a quack. In the end it is the marriage she wants which cures the girl.

THE MISANTHROPE

Molière's genius achieved its highest expression in *The Misanthrope* (1666) and *Tartuffe*. It is part of the paradox of genius that in these two masterpieces the playwright who could fill the stage with such healthy merriment as finds its equal only in Shakespeare, should have been so near the borderline of heart-rending tragedy. For as much as one may be amused by the satirical lines of *The Misanthrope* or *Tartuffe,* no one with a heart is provoked to laughter by either comedy. The truth they present is too bitter, too universal, too near the realm of tears.

The Misanthrope, a verse comedy in five acts, has been called "the French *Hamlet*"—though it is hard to understand on what grounds, unless the comparison is based upon their pre-eminence in their respective literatures. Molière was never closer to reality than in his portraits here: the incorruptible Alceste, who is thoroughly unreasonable; the bewitching but self-centered coquette, Célimène; the insincere man of fashion, Oronte; the urbane but affectionate friend, Philinte; the sensible, good woman, Éliante; and the pretender-to-virtue, mischievous Arsinoë.

Though it had some success when first performed in Paris, it did not please the public as much as the author's earlier farces. But the discriminating at once perceived that he had in this work exceeded in excellence all he had previously written.

The observations of the great French critic, Hippolyte Taine, are well worth quoting: "A dozen conversations constitute the play of *The Misanthrope.* . . . [Such] pieces are made out of nothing. They require no incidents. They find ample scope within the confines of a single room and a single day. . . . This bareness of materials throws out the ideas with more clarity and speed. . . . At every step the clarity increases, the impression is deeper, and vice is silhouetted; the ridicule is heaped until . . . laughter forces it way and breaks out. This laughter is no mere outburst of amusement; it is the judgment which causes it. . . . The writer is a philosopher, who connects us with universal truth by a particular case. . . . We philosophize with him on humanity; because he has thought, we think. . . . None who have tried to show us Man, have conducted us by a more direct or easier route to a sharper and more life-like portrait. I add, to a more pleasing portrait—this is the main talent of comedy, refraining from exhibiting what is hateful. . . . Amusement flees before anger and moralizing. . . . In *The Misanthrope,* is not the sight of a loyal, sincere, honest man, very much in love, whom his virtue eventually overwhelms with ridicule and expels from society, a sorrowful spectacle? . . . . But how everything changes when in the hands of this mercurial Frenchman! how human ugliness is blotted out! how amusing is the entertainment Molière has prepared for us. . . . On canvas, at least, we have a cheerful world. . . . In Molière truth is at the basis, but it lies hidden. He has overheard the sobs of human tragedy, but prefers not to reproduce them. . . . Let us make more lively our state with gaiety, easy talk, and light wit, as we would a sick-room. . . . Let Alceste be grumpy and gauche. . . . It will be amusing. His mishaps will fail to make him a martyr to justice; they will merely be the effects of a contrary-minded character. . . . Molière is the only man who gives us models without pedantry, . . . without solemnity."

For his study of Alceste, Molière must have drawn upon his self-knowledge. His hero's jealous love for the spoiled charmer, Célimène, was perhaps his own vented jealousy and love of his wife, and Alceste's struggle to free himself from his enslaved feelings to one he knows unworthy was perhaps no other than an echo of Molière's own struggle.

It has been maintained that Molière had some particular noblemen in mind in the satire of this play, as well as certain admirers of his wife (who included the Count de Guiche, the Abbé de Richelieu, and the Duke de Lauzun). This is also the only play of its author which implies criticism of Louis XIV, for in attacking Louis' officers he was really attacking the monarch who had appointed them.

THE MISANTHROPE

Le Misanthrope

SCENE: *Célimène's house in Paris*

Persons of the Drama

Alceste: *in love with Célimène*
Philinte: *his friend*
Oronte: *in love with Célimène*
Célimène: *beloved by Alceste*
Éliante: *her cousin*
Arsinoë: *Célimène's friend*
Acaste ⎱
Clitandre ⎰ *marquises*
Basque: *servant to Célimène*
Dubois: *servant to Alceste*
An Officer of the Maréchaussée

ACT I. Alceste (the Misanthrope) is upbraiding his close friend Philinte for being a hypocrite like the rest of the world, just because Philinte doesn't go about telling everyone exactly what he thinks. Alceste would spare no one his evaluation; Philinte says that under some conditions such

lain speaking is intolerable. He laughs and says that the
differences between the two of them remind him of the two
brothers who are so different in *The School for Husbands*.
He pleads for a little more tolerance of the weaknesses of
human nature.

Oronte comes in, assuring Alceste of his great affection
for him, and then, despite his receiving no encouragement,
reads him an idiotic lyric to "Phillis," which Oronte has composed. Philinte praises the lines politely, much to Alceste's
fury. But Oronte will have Alceste's criticism too. Alceste
replies in what for him is tactful roundaboutness: he was telling someone the other day that we ought always "control
the itch for writing which attacks all of us sometimes," that
we should refrain from exhibiting such effusions publicly in
order not to seem foolish, that poetry without feeling is a
bore; he moreover asked this unnamed friend what pressing
need was there for him to write verse? Oronte asks whether
all this is to apply to him. ALCESTE: "I don't say that." Then
how does Alceste feel about Oronte's poem? Alceste's honest
advice is to put it away: he has been following the wretched
models of the day with all their absurd affectations. Then he
sings an old love-song, which, in its sincerity, is far superior
to all these modern offenses against good sense. Oronte leaves
in a huff, and Alceste renews his attack on what he thinks of
as Philinte's hypocrisy. He is utterly disgusted with everyone
and wishes to be left to himself.

ACT II. Célimène is alone with Alceste. He accuses her
of encouraging the attentions of everybody. He confesses that
he would give anything not to love her so passionately as he
does. "Why do I love you so much? Ah, if ever I escape
whole out of your hands, I shall bless Heaven for that good
fortune. I won't lie to you. I do all I can to tear this wretched

devotion from my heart. . . . It is for my sins I am forced to love you this way." She mocks him for the strangeness of his love-speeches.

Two noblemen, Acaste and Clitandre, come in with Éliante [Célimène's cousin] and Philinte. The nobles begin to gossip about their various good friends with elaborate sarcasm, but with a little encouragement from them Célimène outdoes them both in the mercilessness of her satire: Cléonte's manners are too absurd; Damon manages to communicate nothing at great length; Timante is full of grimaces and always has a secret to whisper; Géralde never mixes with any but the highest society, according to him, and talks of nothing but his horses, carriages, and dogs; Bélise is a stupid block and her visits are interminable; Adraste is puffed up with self-conceit; Damis is one of Célimène's closest friends, but he pretends to too much wit, etc. Alceste is enraged to hear the girl he loves behaving like this, and blames her visitors for encouraging her.

ALCESTE: No, madam, now. Though I perish for it, you have amusements which I cannot bear. People are wicked to encourage you in the very faults for which they blame you.

CLITANDRE: I cannot speak for myself. But I can openly declare that up to now I've always deemed this lady without a fault.

ACASTE: I perceive the charms and graces with which she is endowed. But I have never noticed any faults.

Nevertheless, although Alceste feels the others are waiting for him to leave, he is determined to outstay them. But just then an Officer appears to tell him that the Marshal's office wishes to see him on account of his recent disagreement with Oronte over the verses. ALCESTE: "How will they [the officials] settle this? Will the edict of those gentlemen require me to approve of the verses . . . ? I won't take back what I've said. I think them terrible." He goes out, promising to return.

ACT III. Clitandre and Acaste decide to find out which of them is Célimène's favored lover; they agree that the unlucky one will quit the field. As they leave, Arsinoë, the prude, vain of her reputation for virtue, comes in. She tells Célimène that all of Paris is gossiping about the number of admirers she allows to surround her. Célimène answers: She was at a house the other day when some excellent people turned the conversation upon Arsinoë; they didn't approve of Arsinoë's "affectation of a grave air," her "endless talk about wisdom and honor." What is the good of all that? they asked. "She says her prayers devoutly, but she beats her servants and pays them nothing. She shows great piety in every church, but she paints and would try to pass as a beauty. She covers the nakedness in her pictures, but loves the reality." Célimène adds that Arsinoë must not blame her if the latter has no admirers at all; she's not responsible for Arsinoë's advanced age.

When Alceste returns, Célimène leaves him to Arsinoë's wiles. She, as everyone knows, is smitten with Alceste, and does not now conceal her infatuation. But he is not interested in her. She tries to flatter him on talents which have not been sufficiently recognized, but that makes no impression on him.

ARSINOË: Although Célimène is my friend, I don't hesitate to call her unworthy of the heart of a man of honor. She only feigns responding to your affection.

ALCESTE: That's quite possible, madam. . . . But your charity might well have restrained the desire to awake such suspicions in my heart.

He asks to be told plainly what she means. She ends by telling him that if he will accompany her home she will prove to him that Célimène is unworthy of his love.

ACT IV. Philinte tells Éliante how the difficulty between Oronte and Alceste was settled. Alceste refused to alter his opinion that Oronte's verses were execrable. But was that any reflection on Oronte's character; a perfect gentleman may write wretched verses? Finally, Alceste was got to concede that he *wished* he could admire Oronte's verses a little more. That ended the dispute. Philinte and Éliante are unhappy over Alceste's love for Célimène, and know he must eventually be hurt by her. Philinte, guessing that Éliante is herself in love with Alceste without Alceste's returning her affection, tells her that once her feelings for his friend have been liberated, he himself would be honored if she consented to marry him.

Alceste comes in, in a rage because of a letter Arsinoë has put in his possession, a letter written to Oronte by Célimène with a great show of affection. Out of revenge, Alceste proposes marriage to Éliante: "Avenge me on an ungrateful and treacherous relative of yours. . . . Avenge me for an act that should fill you with loathing." ÉLIANTE: "How?" ALCESTE: "By accepting my heart. . . . I shall punish her by the sincere devotion and profound love . . . which I will henceforth offer at your altar."

Before the girl can reply Célimène enters. Proudly and defiantly she refuses to explain her letter to Oronte, and tells Alceste he may believe whatever he chooses, since her assurance that she loves only him isn't sufficient for him. He doesn't deserve the love she has for him. He laments his infatuation; but he feels he must submit to his fate. She, on the other hand, retorts that he is only proving how little he loves her.

A servant comes in to announce that a friend has left a

letter for Alceste at his home, warning him to fly Paris for his life.

ACT V. Alceste tells Philinte that his enemy in a lawsuit which has been pending, has won the case by pulling political strings, even though the world knows that justice was on Alceste's side. Philinte tries to console him by assuring him that his enemy has not succeeded in getting him arrested or in convincing the world by circulating false rumors; the apparent success will damage the adversary more than Alceste. But Alceste had made up his mind to run away from all society, and has come to learn Célimène's decision about him.

Oronte comes in. He is also determined that she make a choice. But she refuses to answer him on the grounds that it would be too indelicate to do so. It is not that she doesn't know whom she prefers, but she is too confused to speak openly before them both. A lover ought to be sensitive to a woman's gentle intimations that his suit is not favored, without having to be told so coarsely. Alceste demands an open statement from her, and Oronte seconds him. Éliante, entering, agrees that the men have a right to know where they stand.

Now Acaste, Clitandre, Philinte, and Arsinoë are also present. ARSINOË: "No doubt you're surprised to see me, madam; but these gentlemen . . . came to see me, and complained of treatment I could scarcely believe. I have too high an estimate of your goodness of heart to believe you capable of such crimes . . . I've been induced to come with them to hear you refute this scandal." The noblemen both have letters from Célimène in which the characters of each other, as well as of Oronte and Alceste, are slandered, and in which each is led to believe that he is the favored suitor.

After being thus exposed, Célimène hears each of the

other three suitors disclaim any further interest in her. They leave. Arsinoë upbraids her on Alceste's behalf, but he tells Arsinoë to mind her own business. He adds: "If I ever decided to avenge myself by choosing another woman, it would not be you." She goes out angrily.

Despite the revelation of her perfidy, Alceste is still willing to marry Célimène if she will go off with him to a desert. CÉLIMÈNE: "I renounce the world before I'm old, and bury myself in your desert?" She flatly refuses to marry him unless he agrees to remain in town for the future. He now rejects her as utterly empty and worthless. He tells Éliante that although he has always admired her, he now feels that he was not cut out for the married state. But she interrupts him. He is, in any case, too late: she has already accepted Philinte's love.

Poisoned against humanity, he runs off, beside himself with rage against the world; he will seek to "find some small secluded place where it will be possible to enjoy the freedom of being an honest man." Philante and Éliante, constant in their affection for him, will try to dissuade him, they say, as they follow him.

◆ Philinte, who urges moderation in all things, is plainly a spokesman for Molière.

This great play has not pleased everyone. Though Jean Jacques Rousseau's own morbidity might have been supposed to make him appreciate the play, he objected to Molière's having made Alceste ridiculous. As for Philinte, who is supposed to be admirable, his opinions "are pretty much those of a scoundrel—one of those gentle and mild optimists who are pleased with everything and everybody," said Rousseau.

On the other hand, Goethe said: "Molière is so great that one is astounded all over again every time one reads him . . .

His pieces border on tragedy." *The Misanthrope* was a particular favorite of his.

Wycherley adapted much of this play in his successful comedy, *The Plain Dealer,* in which, however, all the refinement of Molière's touch has been lost.

DOCTOR IN SPITE OF HIMSELF

In August of 1666 Molière presented a deliriously funny play, *Doctor in Spite of Himself,* a three-act work in prose, which attacks the incompetence of the medical profession. It was based on one of the old French *fabliaux,* which was also the source in modern times for Anatole France's rollicking farce, *The Man Who Married a Dumb Wife.* Molière must also have been familiar with a sprightly passage in Rabelais on the same story.

In *Pantagruel* Rabelais tells how he and some of his friends when they were young took part in a comedy of the man who had married a dumb wife. "The good honest fellow, her spouse, was very anxious to have the filament tying her tongue to be untied. At no matter what cost he wished to hear her speak. At his request, some pains were taken with her; part by work of the physician, part by ingenuity of the surgeon, the ligament under her tongue was cut, she spoke, and went on speaking. Indeed, within a few hours she spoke so loudly, so much, so vehemently and at such length, that her poor husband sought out the same physician for some means to keep her quiet. 'There are,' says the physician, 'many proper remedies in our art to make dumb women speak, but I've never heard of one to keep them silent. The only cure I know of is their husband's deafness.' The poor man, a few weeks later, through the use of drugs, charms, and enchantments which the physician prescribed, became so deaf that he would not have been able to hear the thunder of nineteen hundred cannons shot off at once. His wife, seeing that he was in fact as deaf as a post and that her chiding of him was useless (since he couldn't hear her), grew stark staring mad. Later the physician asked for his fee, to which the husband answered that he was deaf and couldn't understand what the doctor wanted. At that the doctor sprinkled him with some sort of powder, which made him an idiot at once. . . . Then this fool of a husband and his crazy wife joined forces, fell on the physician and the surgeon, and so scratched, beat and banged them that they were left for half dead. . . ."

The Sganarelle of this comedy is more universal than his predecessors. His type can be found today in many a bar or pub: the man who supplements a certain amount of native intelligence with a scattering of polysyllabic words, and who is the hero of his drinking-companions. *Doctor in Spite of Himself* is a delicious farce of infectious mirth. Many English dramatists have adapted it for their own purposes.

Molière again enacted the role of Sganarelle, this time a drunken woodcutter who abuses his wife.

DOCTOR IN SPITE
OF HIMSELF

Le Médecin malgré Lui

Persons of the Drama

Géronte: *father to Lucinde*
Léandre: *Lucinde's lover*
Sganarelle: *husband to Martine*
Monsieur Robert: *Sganarelle's neighbor*
Lucas: *husband to Jacqueline*
Valère: *Géronte's servant*
Thibaut ⎫
Perrin: *his son* ⎰ *peasants*
Lucinde: *Géronte's daughter*
Martine: *Sganarelle's wife*
Jacqueline: *nurse at Géronte's, and Lucas' wife*

ACT I. A forest. Sganarelle and his wife, Martine, enter quarrelling, each wishing to dominate the other. He quotes a non-existent passage from Aristotle against wives in general, and boasts his cleverness. Where will one find another wood-cutter who can hold forth in argument or one who has served a doctor for six years, and who since infancy had his "rudiments" of learning at his fingertips? They blame each other for being ungrateful at the great fortune of being able to marry such a spouse. She accuses him of eating her out of hearth and home; he calls that a lie: he *drinks* part of it. She accuses him further of selling all their household goods, and of using the proceeds to drink and gamble. MARTINE: "I've got four little children on my hands." HE: "Put them down." She increases her indictment against him until, beyond patience, he beats her with a stick. She screams for help.

Their neighbor, Robert, comes running in. He upbraids Sganarelle for beating his wife and his thanks is to get a slap in the face from her. SHE: "I like him to beat me." She proceeds to harangue Robert for not minding his own business. He apologizes to Sganarelle; he, too, gives his neighbor a whack with his stick for good measure. SGANARELLE: "I'll beat her if I like, and I won't if I don't." Robert runs out. Sganarelle urges his wife to make it up, and they forgive each other. He goes off to work. She decides to get even with him.

Valère (Géronte's servant) and Lucas (Jacqueline's husband) come in. They do not at first see Martine. They are both concerned about the illness of their master's daughter, Lucinde. While she is sick there can be no question of her getting married. She favors Léandre, but her father would never consent to that match. LUCAS: "But what sort of idea is this which he has taken into his head since the doctors have run out of their Latin expressions?" Martine, still planning vengeance on her husband, at last notices the newcomers. They tell her that they were sent to find some particularly clever doctor to bring relief to Lucinde, since she has through illness lost the use of her tongue. Several physicians have already failed, and their master wants them to find another one. This gives Martine an idea. She declares: "We have a man here who's the most remarkable in the world for cases that have been declared hopeless." She tells them that they'll find him a little further on in the forest. A doctor who cuts wood? MARTINE: "He's an odd fellow . . . a strange, fantastic, eccentric man . . . He goes about dressed in a most unusual way—sometimes pretending to be an ignoramus . . . There's nothing he dislikes more than using the wonderful talent God has given him as a healer. . . . But this man's obsessions are beyond imagining. Occasionally he has to be beaten . . . He'll never admit he's a doctor unless you take a stick to him and cudgel him into admitting it." Martine goes out.

Sganarelle is heard singing behind the scenes, and comes out with a bottle in his hand. Lucas and Valère realize he is the doctor they are seeking. They are very circumspect in raising the subject of their search; they would talk of cures, he talks of cut logs. Valère expresses his disgust that a celebrated medico should take on such a disguise and bury his talents. When they boldly declare him to be a physician, he denies it. They realize that they have to apply the remedy; each takes a stick and thrashes him. He tentatively admits that he is a doctor; when he begins to retract, they thrash him again. That is enough and he loudly affirms his being a doctor. They are quick to apologize for the harsh treatment they were obliged to use. Are they *quite* certain he's a doctor? They are ready to swear he is, and recount the great cures of which Martine has told them. He is astounded to hear of his amazing accomplishments—such as bringing back to life a woman who had been dead for hours and healing immediately a child who had fallen from a belfry. They beg him to accompany them to see the girl who cannot talk. They promise to get him a physician's gown, which he lacks, and think him an amiable jokester for a physician.

ACT II. A room in Géronte's house. Valère and Lucas assure Géronte that they've now got Lucinde the greatest doctor in the world—although one would have to admit that he has a screw loose somewhere. Jacqueline, Lucas' wife, offers the opinion that all the girl needs is a handsome, strapping fellow for a husband. Géronte rejects the advice; how can his daughter marry with her present affliction? And why did she reject the husband he chose for her? JACQUELINE: Why didn't he give her the man she likes, Léandre, who'd take her as she is? Géronte won't have him for a son-in-law because he's not rich enough. Jacqueline reminds her master that Léandre's uncle is wealthy; anyhow, she adds, "I'd rather give my daughter a husband she wants than have all the country's wealth." Her husband and Géronte bid her hold her tongue.

Sganarelle is brought in, wearing a physician's gown and pointed cap. He thinks Géronte is a doctor and begins to quote Hippocrates. When Géronte declares he's not a doctor, Sganarelle beats him, declaring: "Now you're a physician. This is the only degree I've had myself." Géronte is indignant, but his servants remind him that this learned man is an eccentric.

Lucas and Jacqueline (who is Lucinde's nurse) come in. Sganarelle envies the child that has sucked those handsome bosoms, and begins to caress them. Lucas pulls him away, and has a task keeping him separated from Jacqueline. Sganarelle says that he'll like to test the nurse's milk and examine her breasts, but Lucas strongly objects.

The patient comes in. Géronte says he'd never get over it if this, his only child, dies. SGANARELLE: "She mustn't die without a doctor's prescription." Lucinde cannot refrain from laughing—a good sign. Sganarelle questions her about her symptoms, and she replies in pantomine and unintelligible sounds. Géronte says that her appointed husband is waiting for her recovery to marry her. SGANARELLE: "Who is this idiot who doesn't want his wife speechless? I wish to Heaven mine were." Sganarelle takes her pulse, and concludes from it that she is speechless. Géronte would like to know the cause of her dumbness. SGANARELLE: "It comes from her loss of speech." He then begins to talk of "humors," "vapors," "exhalations," and other commonplaces of medicine. Does Géronte know Latin? No. He's sure? He doesn't know a word. In that case Sganarelle is ready to speak in that tongue, which he does in part gibberish and part phrases from an old Latin grammar. Géronte, impressed, regrets his own lack of education. When Sganarelle begins to talk of the liver and the heart and to examine them, however, Géronte is compelled to remark that the doctor's hands seem to place them on the wrong side of the body. SGANARELLE: "That was true formerly. We're changed all that. Nowadays we doctors practise according to a new system." His counsel is that Lucinde be put to bed and given plenty of bread soaked in wine; that will tend to bring back her speech.

He detains Jacqueline, saying he would like to administer some medicine to her. She counters: I'm in perfect health. HE: "So much the worse, so much the worse. This excess of good health is dangerous." She had better be bled for the diseases she may yet have. But she will have none of that. Géronte wishes to pay Sganarelle for his services; the would-be doctor at first pretends to reject, but then accepts, the money.

Léandre comes in, saying he needs the doctor's help—not for his health, but in a stratagem to win Lucinde. Sganarelle loudly protests the insult to his profession—until Léandre takes out his purse. Lucinde's sweetheart tells the mock-doctor that, despite the arguments of the physicians, her illness is all pretended. She has invented it to escape the marriage her father wishes to force upon her. Sganarelle is now interested:

"If my medical knowledge does not fail me, the sick girl shall either die or be yours."

ACT III.   A spot near Géronte's house. Léandre in a new wig is got up as an apothecary, and asks Sganarelle to supply him with a few medical terms. The false doctor declares such knowledge superfluous. He ends by confessing the truth about himself to Lucinde's lover. He doesn't know how, but now everyone comes running to him for his medical assistance, though his education terminated during his first year of schooling. But the profession of doctor is the best trade of all, he has found: whether a doctor does well or ill, he is paid just the same. A shoemaker would not be excused for his blunders. But if a man dies, it's never the doctor's fault, only the patient's. And the dead are too honest to speak up and reveal the facts.

Thibaut, a peasant, and his son Perrin come seeking the doctor. Thibaut's wife has been sick abed for six months. They want her cured. She is sick, they say, "with the hypocrisy." She is swollen all over. They begin to give a garbled version of the medical terms generally in use. Sganarelle shows little interest until they pay him in advance. On the basis of their description of her symptoms he prescribes "a prepared cheese containing gold, coral, and pearls." They go off to get it for her. SGANARELLE: "And if she dies, don't forget to bury her in style."

The scene now changes to the room of Act II. Delighted to see Jacqueline again, Sganarelle begs her to become ill so he can cure her, and inveighs against the jealousy of her husband. He is about to embrace her when Lucas intervenes, and the two go off in opposite directions.

Sganarelle comes in with Léandre as an apothecary. How is the patient? Much worse, says Géronte. So much the better, opines the doctor; it shows that the medicine is working. He introduces the apothecary.

Jacqueline brings in Lucinde, whose pulse the apothecary proceeds to take. While the doctor keeps Géronte busy with learned comments, the lovers are able to have a whispered conference. Suddenly Géronte hears his daughter speaking out in an unguarded moment. He is overjoyed and deeply in the doctor's debt. But Lucinde uses her recovered powers to assure her father: "I'll marry no one but Léandre." She continues talking with energy, vows she'll enter a convent rather than wed her father's choice, and gives her father not one chance to utter a syllable. Frustrated, Géronte, unable to stand her torrent of words, asks the doctor to make her dumb again. Sganarelle says that is impossible; "all I can do for you is to make you deaf." Still unable to render his daughter obedient, Géronte appeals to the doctor. This is a new disease, says Sganarelle, and he can cure it. He takes the apothecary aside and warns him that a remedy for Lucinde must be found at once; he recommends "a dose of purgative flight mixt with two drams of matrimonium." The apothecary may have some trouble getting the girl to swallow this pill; he'd better take a turn in the garden to convince her. The lovers go out.

Géronte, still fuming over his daughter's insolence, tells the doctor how he has kept Léandre and her apart. Lucas comes in to inform them that Léandre has fled with Lucinde; it was he who was the apothecary. Sganarelle would like to sneak out, but Lucas detains him, while Géronte goes out to get a magistrate. Martine has at last caught up with her husband, and learns from Lucas that he is to be hanged.

Géronte comes back, soon followed by Lucinde and Léandre. Léandre has decided against an elopement. He wishes to receive Lucinde honorably from her father's hands. Moreover, his uncle has just died and he has fallen heir to a large fortune. This last piece of information converts Géronte. He gives his daughter to her lover with the greatest pleasure. Sganarelle is forgiven, and he tells his wife that henceforth he must be treated with more respect because of his elevation in life.

MÉLICERTE

In December of 1666 Molière presented, among other pieces, Mélicerte, a two-act "heroic pastoral comedy" in verse, which much pleased the King. Its plot revolves about a double interchange of children. It is of small interest now.

THE SICILIAN

The next month he gave the charming comedy-ballet, The Sicilian, in alternate prose and verse, also before the King at St. Germain-en-Laye—a piece much admired by Voltaire. The plot, which Beaumarchais kept in mind when writing The Barber of Seville, has to do with Adraste's deception of Don Pedro, when he introduces himself into the latter's household as a painter who is going to do a portrait of Isidore, Don Pedro's zealously guarded ward, and how he rescues her from her guardian's tyranny. Adraste's sister, Climène, speaks the moral at the end: jealousy is abhorred by all sane people; "the heart must be won by sweetness and charm."

◆ Overwork and a severe cold he had caught began to undermine Molière's health, and the first symptoms of consumption began to manifest themselves in him. A gazette of the time reported in April of 1667 that his life was in danger; nevertheless, less than two months later he was appearing in a play before the King.

AMPHITRYON

On January 13, 1668, he produced the three-act verse comedy, *Amphitryon*, a very free adaptation from Plautus. There has been some dispute as to whether in this play the dramatist intended to ridicule M. de Montespan, husband of the King's new mistress; but the fact that Louis XIV, later in life, when under the pious influence of Mme. de Maintenon, continued to enjoy seeing this fairly coarse play would indicate that the monarch saw in it no personal references. If Molière had the King and the royal libido in mind, he was certainly extraordinarily reckless in writing such a work.

In Greek legend, Amphitryon had to wife Alcmene. Zeus, assuming the form of her husband, slept with Alcmene, who on successive days bore his son Hercules, and after that Amphitryon's son Iphicles. Plautus' play, the only burlesque surviving from Latin comedy, was a burlesque of the story.

AMPHITRYON

SCENE: *Thebes, before the house of Amphitryon*

Persons of the Drama

Mercury
Night
Jupiter: *who appears under the form of Amphitryon*
Amphitryon: *general of the Thebans*
Alcmène: *Amphitryon's wife*
Cléanthis: *Alcmène's attendant and Sosie's wife*
Sosie: *Amphitryon's valet*

Argatiphontidas ⎫
Naucratès   ⎬ *Theban captains*
Polidas   ⎪
Posiclès   ⎭

PROLOGUE. Mercury is on a cloud; Night is in a chariot drawn by two horses. Mercury informs Night that Jupiter wishes the aid of her cloak for a new love-affair he intends to prosecute. While Amphitryon is away commanding the Theban troops, Jupiter has assumed his form; even though Amphitryon and Alcmène have been married only a few days, Jupiter's lust could be satisfied only by possessing Alcmène. Night marvels at all of Jupiter's disguises, but Mercury approves of them: In my view "there is nothing more idiotic than always being imprisoned in one's grandeur; besides, lofty rank is highly inconvenient to the transports of amorous desire. Jupiter, as a connoisseur of pleasure, knows how to come down from the heights of his supreme glory." But Night wishes to know: since Jupiter has been successful in taking his place in Alcmène's bed, what more does he wish? That Night slacken her horses, is the reply, so that Jupiter may have the longest night of all for his love-making. As for Mercury, he is about to strip himself of his form too, and take on the figure of Amphitryon's valet. Mercury descends from his cloud and Night drives off in her chariot.

ACT I. Sosie, Amphitryon's valet, has been sent by his master to announce his return, night-time though it is, and to give Alcmène a full description of his military victory. Sosie practices his speech in advance.

Mercury, looking like Sosie's identical twin, comes in. Sosie doesn't like his face. Mercury challenges him as though Sosie were the stranger to the house, refuses to allow him to enter, and beats him, warning him he will keep it up until the other stops insisting that *he* is Sosie. By recounting Amphitryon's victory and rattling off the names of Sosie's family and progenitors, Mercury soon has Sosie wondering about his own identity. But if Mercury is Sosie, who is Sosie himself? Mercury promises him that when he ceases being Sosie, Sosie can again be himself. Finding his way into the house still barred, the real Sosie runs away.

Jupiter (in the form of Amphitryon) enters with Alcmène, and tells her that no lights must be brought yet; he doesn't want it known that he has left the battlefield to steal home to his wife. Cryptically he says: "The love and tenderness I feel for you far exceeds that of a husband." He must leave her now, and he bids her "think of the lover when you see the husband." Cléanthis, Alcmène's servant and wife to Sosie, envies her mistress the tenderness of such a husband; her own is nothing like this.

Mercury, prepared to inform Night that she may allow the Sun to rise, is stopped on his way out by Cléanthis, who chides him for the little passion Sosie has shown for her. She wishes, because of his indifference, that she were not an honest woman.

ACT II. Sosie is telling the real Amphitryon of his encounter with the other Sosie. "Another me . . . This me was at your house before me. I swear to you that that me was there before me." Amphitryon cannot make head or tail of the story. He tries to convince Sosie that he is talking nonsense. When his valet tells him of the thrashing he got, Amphitryon asks who administered it. SOSIE: "Myself . . . Not the me who is here, but the me from the house."

Alcmène and Cléanthis come out. Amphitryon greets her, and hopes this day will be favorable to his passion. She is astounded to see him returned so soon. Her husband, hurt, says he expected a different greeting—after what seemed to him an interminable absence. She reminds him that he left her at break of day; he thinks she must have been dreaming. SHE: Can he have already forgot all the love she has just lavished on him? Each thinks the other is jesting. Can he deny that he arrived early the previous night? Can she deny that she hasn't seen him until now? How, she asks, could she otherwise have a full account of his military victories, as she has? And what about the cluster of diamonds he sent her? He is amazed, when she shows him the jewels. Sosie says this is a joke; because he was refused admission to the house he still has the gift his master sent. The valet opens the casket and finds the diamonds gone. Now, Alcmène demands of her husband, can you still say you were not here? She bids him remember the joy with which she greeted him and how she showed that joy "more than once." Never was her husband so tender and so passionate. They supped alone, she reminds him, and then went to bed. Amphitryon bitterly exclaims that it was not he who went to bed with her. He accuses her of betraying him, and he vows revenge. On whom? she asks. She decides that he is playing a role in order to break their marriage: he needn't be at such pains, for she is ready to agree. Though unsure of the details, Amphitryon knows he has been a victim of treachery; her brother can vouch for the fact that they kept company until morning. He goes off in a rage, and she returns in tears to the house.

Cléanthis starts abusing Sosie, because of the way Mercury treated her. On his return with his master last night, Sosie (actually Mercury) rejected her tenderness and was as cold as ice, and refused to go to bed with her, as was plainly his marital duty.

Jupiter returns with the purpose of easing Alcmène's sorrow; he will take the opportunity for a renewed indulgence of his passion. He goes upstairs to her. But she is soon downstairs again, Jupiter following her. She tells him that she now regards him as a frightful monster, and that he is odious in her sight. His harsh words have killed her love. She could have forgiven him if his outburst had been due to jealousy. He interrupts her to admit that he was guilty: it was the husband who wounded her, not the lover. If she must be avenged, let her hate the husband and love the lover. These subtleties, she says, are too much for her. Since she will not pardon him, he offers her his sword and asks her to run him through. By degrees he assuages her anger, and ends by conducting her off to bed again. He tells Sosie to invite some Theban captains to dinner.

Sosie is inspired to go to bed with his wife, but she will have none of him.

ACT III.   Amphitryon is only annoyed at all the congratulations he has been receiving for his military successes, while his mind is so disturbed about his wife. He decides to question her again about the facts. Mercury comes in, determined to have some fun at Amphitryon's expense. He answers to the name of Sosie, and pretends not to recognize the master of the house. Amphitryon, he says, is at this minute lying by the side of his beautiful Alcmène; they have become reconciled after their recent tiff and are enjoying the pleasures of love. Amphitryon is in despair.

The real Sosie comes in with two Theban captains he has found for his master, Naucratès and Polidas. Amphitryon begins to beat Sosie for his insults of a few minutes ago and his refusal to open the door of the house. Sosie reminds his master that he had been bidden to invite these captains to dinner. Amphitryon feels himself going mad. Naucratès advises him to attempt clearing up the whole matter before letting himself get into a rage.

Jupiter comes down, wishing to know what all the noise is about. Amphitryon is astounded to see his double. Jupiter promises them all to clear up the mystery, and the captains are already convinced that Jupiter is the real Amphitryon. Amphitryon himself goes out to find friends to support his claims. Sosie, in the meantime, has another passage of confused identity with *his* double, Mercury.

Amphitryon arrives with two other captains, Argatiphontidas and Posiclès. Cléanthis, entering, is astonished to see that besides the Amphitryon in the house there is one outside.

Mercury comes in to announce to all present that the Amphitryon within is none other than "the great master of the Gods," and that he himself is the god Mercury, who, tired of Sosie's ugly face, is happy to give it up. He flies off to the skies.

Jupiter now appears in a cloud, identifies himself, confesses what he has done. His being the father of the gods, the exploit "stifles all possible scandal." Alcmène and Amphitryon have been in no way dishonored; he must feel it a glory to have a god for a rival, and ought to be gratified that only by masquerading as her husband could Jupiter win Alcmène's favors. Sosie compliments Jupiter for knowing how to sugar-coat a bitter pill. Jupiter also prophesies the birth of his son Hercules, whose deeds shall be celebrated all over the world.

The embarrassed captains try to congratulate Amphitryon, who remains silent, but Sosie, who has the last speech, counsels: "In affairs like these it's always best to say nothing."

GEORGE DANDIN

On July 18, 1668 Molière presented his three-act prose comedy, *George Dandin,* written for festivities at Versailles, where, for the occasion, each of the acts alternated with a pastoral-opera-comedy-ballet, the music composed by the distinguished composer Lully, the words by Molière.

The name, Dandin, now commonly used to signify a booby, originates in Rabelais. The plot of the play itself has as its source Stories 4 and 8 of the Seventh Day of the *Decameron*. The comedy was later performed in Paris, where the audiences were not unfamiliar with the wealthy peasant who has married into the nobility and the impoverished noble who has only his pride left.

The action of the play shows George Dandin, the peasant, who is informed by an unknown man that his wife is listening with favor to the advances of a young nobleman in love with her. He complains to her parents, a pair of moneyless people of exalted rank, of this infidelity and accuses their daughter of breaking the vows she took at the marriage-altar. George Dandin now tortures himself with remorse over his folly in having wed into the aristocracy. His wife presently speaks to him with such arrogance as makes him despair. Soon, to fill up his cup with bitterness, he learns that his wife is in his house with her gallant. He hastens to inform his father-in-law and mother-in-law of this new development. But his wife manages to justify herself to her parents and, taking a stick, beats her husband with it instead of her gallant whom she pretends to be maltreating. But poor Dandin has yet more to suffer. His wife goes out at night with her gallant. When she returns, her husband refuses to open the door for her. Because of her fear of her father and mother, whom he has sent for as witnesses to the event, she pleads for admission into the house in the tenderest terms. But he persists in his refusal until she pretends that she is about to commit suicide. He comes down with a taper to see whether she has actually carried out her threat; she has concealed herself, and at the opportune moment steals into the house. She convinces her parents that her husband is drunk, with the result that her father, after many threats, forces George Dandin to beg his wife's forgiveness. Dandin, after suffering all this disgrace, concludes that "when one has, like me, wed a wicked woman, the best thing one can do is to drown himself."

The story thus has two themes: that of the deceived

husband and that of the peasant misled by the desire to elevate his rank. The portraits of his wife's father and mother, the de Sotenvilles, are masterful. But the comedy in this play is fairly sour since none of the other characters evoke our sympathy— neither Dandin, nor his faithless Angélique, nor the cold-hearted seducer Clitandre.

THE MISER

This play was followed on September 9, 1668 by one of its author's most important comedies, *The Miser,* a five-act prose adaptation of Plautus' *Aulularia.* Molière played the role of Harpagon, whose very name has since become synonymous with the disease of miserliness, perhaps the most obnoxious of all mental illnesses. This bitter comedy shows the mischief which avarice can work within a family. Harpagon is a man fabulously rich who, while adding to his store by usury, re-fuses to part with a penny of it. His name comes from the Latin *harpago,* "a grappling hook," suggesting a man who grasps everything within reach; the names of his servants have been equally well chosen: La Flèche ("arrow"), La Merluche ("stockfish"), and Brindavoine ("stalk-of-oats"), all conveying the idea of their being thin and unfed.

It is strange now to consider that although the literary dictator of the age, Boileau, rated Molière's comedy high above that of the worshiped Plautus, the Parisian public did not at first take to this magnificent play. Possibly its bitterness was too much for them to be amused. However, by degrees the play won its now established place as one of its author's master-pieces.

THE MISER

L'Avare

SCENE: *Harpagon's house in Paris*

Persons of the Drama

Harpagon: *father to Cléante and Élise, and in love with Mariane*

Cléante: *Harpagon's son, and Mariane's lover*

Élise: *Harpagon's daughter, and Valère's lover*

Valère: *Anselme's son, and Élise's lover*

Mariane: *Cléante's lover, and loved by Harpagon*

Anselme: *father to Valère and Mariane*

Frosine: *an intriguer*

Simon: *an agent*

Master Jacques: *cook and coachman to Harpagon*

La Flèche: *Cléante's valet*

Dame Claude: *Harpagon's chambermaid*

Brindavoine ⎫
La Merluche ⎬ *Harpagon's lackeys*

Officer; Officer's Clerk

ACT I. Valère is in love with Élise, Harpagon's daughter. She is worried that her father will never permit their marriage. She has loved Valère ever since he saved her from a death by drowning, when he not only risked his life for her, but treated her with infinite delicacy and consideration. Since then, too, has he not neglected family and country to remain where she is? He himself has no doubt that he can win his own relatives over to their marriage, if he can only find them again. If he does not have news of them soon he will go in search of them. She would prefer his staying on as her father's steward in order to ingratiate himself with her father. He answers that he is making admirable progress in that direction: he has learned that the best way to win affection is to flatter a man's faults and applaud whatever he does. Though he is sacrificing sincerity in behaving so, he feels that the fault is with those who must be flattered. She asks why he does not also try to win the support of her brother, Cléante. Valère replies that he cannot manage both at once; besides father and son are so opposed in disposition that it would be too difficult to be in the confidence of both. Let Élise attempt to win over her brother. Seeing Cléante approaching, Valère leaves.

Cléante confides in his sister his love for Mariane, who lives in circumstances which are most humble. He would wish nothing better from life than to render existence easier for the girl. But his father's avarice makes it impossible for him to taste that joy. Indeed, Cléante continues, Élise cannot imagine how bad things are for him—and all because of his father's meanness. What good will it be to inherit a fortune when one will no longer be of an age to enjoy it? Right now he is forced to borrow money where he can, and at exorbitant rates of interest. He begs his sister to intercede for him with their father to win his approval for a match with Mariane; if Harpagon will not consent, the two lovers will run off somewhere else and trust to fate. Hearing Harpagon's voice, they both quickly go out.

Harpagon comes in, cursing Cléante's valet, La Flèche, ordering him out of the house for being a spy, and for looking around to see what he can rob. Who could rob you, demands La Flèche, when you keep everything locked up? Well, charges Harpagon, wouldn't you be the sort of fellow to spread rumors that I have money hidden all over the house? Have you? asks the valet. Harpagon again orders La Flèche out of the house, but first goes through his pockets to be sure he hasn't hidden anything in them.

Alone, Harpagon complains about the difficulty involved in keeping large sums of money in the house. It's better to have all of it out on interest. A hiding-place is hard to find. He doesn't trust safes: they're only bait to burglars. He has buried ten thousand crowns in the garden, as the best of hiding-places. Élise and Cléante re-enter, and he fears they have heard him talking aloud to himself. He badgers them to discover whether they have heard what he was saying. He begins to plead the shortage of money in these hard times. CLÉANTE: "You have no cause to complain; we know you are rich." Harpagon denies it, and bitterly accuses his children of being in league with his enemies. Cléante's extravagances are such that someday someone will come and cut Harpagon's throat in the belief the house is stuffed with gold pieces, the old man says. He berates his son for dressing too lavishly; he must be robbing him to pay for his clothes. Afraid to tell him the truth about his borrowing from money-lenders, Cléante says that he is lucky at gambling and that he uses his winnings to garb himself. Why doesn't the young man lend out his winnings at interest instead?

Cléante now tells his father that he wants to talk to him about marriage. HARPAGON: "And it's about marriage that I want to talk to you." Have his son and daughter noticed a girl called Mariane, who lives nearby? What does Cléante think

of her? Wouldn't she make a desirable wife? Cléante enthusiastically agrees. There is, however, Harpagon adds, one
important reservation: she has no money. Not important, says
his son airily. Harpagon is willing to admit her other qualities
make up to a degree for this serious impediment; he is glad
that Cléante likes her, for he, Harpagon, has determined to
marry her! Near fainting at this news, Cléante goes out.

Harpagon tells Élise that he is going to marry Cléante to a
certain widow, and that she will marry Monsieur Anselme, a
wealthy man of fifty. She emphatically refuses. He assures her
that she will wed the man of his choice this very evening. She
threatens to kill herself rather than submit. He boasts that the
world will approve of the match, and, seeing Valère approaching, offers to submit the case to him. She agrees to that.

Valère is told of the contention. What is his opinion? He
agrees with both of them. Harpagon will not have this: the
great advantage in this proposed match is that Anselme is
willing to forego any dowry with the bride. Valère says
sarcastically that that ought to settle the question; of course,
Élise might maintain that marriage involves a more important
question—that "of being happy or miserable all one's life";
other people might also say that a daughter's wishes ought to
be consulted and that so great a disparity in age is bound to
lead to catastrophe; but what are such arguments against the
consideration of "no dowry?" Just then Harpagon thinks he
hears a dog barking. Most likely it's someone with designs on
the money buried in the garden. He goes out quickly.

Élise is astonished at Valère's complaisance with her
father. He assures her that the best way to manage him is to
pretend agreement with him; there will always be some way to
defeat his plans: she can ask, for instance, for a delay and
feign illness.

Harpagon comes back; seeing him, Valère at once changes

his tune. Delighted, Harpagon tells him that he wishes Valère to have full control over her. Valère continues to propound the importance of money, with Harpagon's great approval.

ACT II. Cléante tells La Flèche that his own father is now his rival. La Flèche informs his young master that the fifteen thousand francs Cléante desires can be procured from one Simon—but on certain conditions, including interest at the rate of over twenty-five percent, of which Simon as agent will get five and one-half, the usurer twenty percent. Since Cléante needs the money, he feels forced to agree to these outrageous terms. But the lender also stipulates that of the fifteen thousand crowns he can actually give only twelve thousand; the rest will have to be in furniture, clothing, and jewels. Though disgusted, poor Cléante seems to have no other recourse than to accept that condition too. He is reduced to these humiliating experiences by the stinginess of his father. La Flèche declares that it would be almost a meritorious crime to rob Harpagon.

Cléante and La Flèche are at the further end of the stage when Harpagon comes in with Simon, the agent for the usurer. Simon is asking Harpagon for the money to be loaned to Cléante; he cannot identify the client, since La Flèche has not mentioned his young master's name, but Harpagon will be able to meet the young man in question, and ask him anything he wishes: all Simon knows is that he comes from a rich family, and that he can promise his father's demise within eight months. Harpagon is pleased at the last assurance. Cléante, not having overheard the talk, is fearful that La Flèche may have betrayed his name to the agent, and tries to steal off, when Simon sees La Flèche, and introduces Cléante as the would-be-borrower. Harpagon is in wrath, Simon runs out, and La Flèche hides.

Father and son upbraid each other, the former for the

son's extravagance, the latter for the father's sharp practices. Harpagon goes off to take another look at his money.

Frosine, a designing woman, encounters La Flèche, and informs him that she is arranging a small matter for Harpagon, for which she expects to be rewarded. The valet advises her not to count on much. Seeing Harpagon returning, La Flèche leaves.

Frosine flatters Harpagon with the compliment that he looks younger than most people in their mid-twenties. He confesses to being over sixty. She reads his palm and assures him that he will live to be more than a hundred and twenty: he will bury his children's children. HARPAGON: "So much the better!" She is acting as the go-between in the marriage he is planning for himself with Mariane. Has Frosine urged Mariane's mother to dig up some dowry for her daughter's marriage to him? "She must bleed herself, if necessary, for an event like this. After all, you don't marry a girl without her bringing some money." Frosine replies that Mariane will bring plenty of money—since she has been trained to live on vegetables, cheese, and apples, and to do without expensive food and delicacies, clothes or jewels: the savings involved in marrying such a girl will add up to a fortune. Harpagon now expresses his fears at marrying anyone so much younger; won't such a wife seek men of her own age? Mariane, Frosine avers, has an aversion to all except old men. Harpagon enthusiastically endorses such good taste of his prospective bride. Frosine goes on to laud his figure and physique, to his great pleasure. Tactfully Frosine now explains that she herself needs a little money because of a law-suit she is losing. But at that, despite her skill in thrusting in more flattery, Harpagon says, "I must go. Somebody's calling me. Bye, bye." She is in a rage at having been defrauded of her reward.

ACT III. Harpagon is assigning tasks for his servants in advance of a supper he is giving. Claude is to look after the bottles of wine; if one is missing or broken, it will be deducted from her wages. Brindavoine and La Merluche are to fill the glasses only when the guests are thirsty; they are by no means to suggest another drink when none is asked for—and no drink is to be poured until asked for more than once. They are to remember to bring a great deal of water; let the guests fill up on that. They are to stand in a way that will not reveal the holes or stains in their uniforms. Élise is to keep an eye on what is carried away from the table, and see that nothing is wasted. Cléante is to be charming to Mariane; this the boy can honestly promise to be. Harpagon now asks Jacques, the coachman-cook, to dish up something special; that will take money, says Jacques. HARPAGON: "Always money. They seem to speak of nothing else; money, money, money!" Valère seconds Harpagon; a clever man ought to serve something fine with little cost. Jacques offers to change offices with Valère since he seems to possess the secret of buying without money. Harpagon says that there will be eight or ten at table; but Jacques is to count on eight; if there is enough for eight, that will do to serve ten. When Jacques goes over the proposed menu, Harpagon explodes at the number of dishes he intends; Valère reminds Jacques that good health requires spare eating, and undertakes to supervise the supper. As coachman, this same Jacques tells his master that the horses are so undernourished that they are mere ghosts. Harpagon refuses to listen to such tales. In exasperation Jacques indicts his master for his miserliness, rehearses the incredible stratagems to which Harpagon has recourse in order to save money—and is thrashed for his impudence. When his master goes out, Jacques threatens Valère as an upstart, and gets a good drubbing from him too.

Mariane arrives with Frosine; Mariane is in dread of her interview with Harpagon; she makes it plain that she is already smitten with the unknown courteous young man who has visited at her house. Frosine warns against the poverty of young men; better to marry an old man, and after his death take a man of one's choice.

Harpagon comes in and compliments Mariane on her beauty; he is offended that she remains silent. Élise enters, and the two girls greet each other formally. Mariane whispers to Frosine that she finds Harpagon unpleasant. Cléante joins them and Mariane identifies him to Frosine as the suitor of whom she has spoken. Harpagon tells Mariane not to be worried at his having grown-up children; he will be rid of both of them soon. The lovers manage to communicate to each other how much unprepared they were for this encounter; Cléante also openly tells Mariane how much he disapproves of her marriage to his father; she tells him how much she disapproves of having him for a stepson. Harpagon is befuddled by this mixture of politeness and apparent insult. Cléante now says that, putting himself in his father's place, the title of being her husband must turn out to be a glorious one. His praise of her becomes so passionate and extravagant that his father intercedes. Cléante takes a diamond from his father's finger, bids her admire it, and then refuses to allow her to return it; it belongs on her finger, a present he makes in Harpagon's name. Bursting with fury, the old man is forced to suppress his feelings.

A servant enters to announce the arrival of someone with money for Harpagon. The guests are supposed presently to go in Harpagon's coach to see the fair. La Merluche runs in to say that the horses need shoeing. While waiting for these matters to be taken care of, Cléante suggests taking Mariane into the garden, where he will have the refreshments served. As they go out, Harpagon asks Valère to keep his eye on the refreshments, and save as much as possible to be returned to the tradespeople from whom they were purchased.

ACT IV. Élise lets Mariane know that she is in her brother's confidence and is aware of his love for the girl. Frosine regrets that she did not know of this love before. Mariane does not know what to do to avoid marrying Harpagon, and pleads for Cléante's direction; he, in turn, appeals to Frosine. Frosine feels that she could manage Mariane's mother but is not so sure about Harpagon. If he finds himself rejected, he will only refuse to give his consent to Cléante's marrying Mariane. Somehow it must be Harpagon himself who rejects the girl. Frosine has an idea: what if a woman, a little advanced in years, were got up to pose as a noblewoman of wealth who was madly in love with Harpagon, and would settle all her property on him on the day of their marriage? Harpagon loves money more than he could ever love Mariane. Cléante thinks the plan excellent, entreats Frosine's prosecution of it, and asks Mariane to work upon her mother in his behalf. As he is kissing his sweetheart's hand, Harpagon, entering, sees him doing it and is not at all pleased. The ladies are now ready to go in his coach to the fair.

Harpagon questions his son on Mariane. Cléante disparages her beauty and intelligence. The crafty old man wants to know whether the boy has no inclination for her. Cléante has none. Harpagon is sorry to hear that; he's been reconsidering the wisdom of his marrying anyone so much younger, and would have given the girl to his son if the latter had not felt such an aversion to her. Cléante professes his willingness to marry her—just to please his father. No, no good can come of that, says Harpagon; I'll have to go back to my plan of marrying her myself. Disarmed by his tricky father, Cléante now openly confesses his love for Mariane and admits that it began some time ago. At last in full possession of the facts, his father pounces upon him with the announcement that Cléante must get rid of his love, marry the woman Harpagon has chosen for him, and accustom himself to the idea of Mariane as his step-mother. Furious at having been deceived into a full revelation, and to no avail, Cléante denounces his father and swears to continue loving Mariane. Harpagon threatens him.

Jacques comes in, and the two submit the case to him. Hearing both sides, Jacques tries to appease both; to Harpagon he says that Cléante is sorry about his momentary anger, and provided Harpagon will give him someone he can be pleased with as a wife, he is ready to submit; to Cléante he says that Harpagon will do as his son wishes, provided the latter treats his father with respect. Neither has said anything like this to Jacques. Harpagon thus thinks that Cléante is ready to agree to Harpagon's marriage to Mariane, Cléante that Harpagon is ready to agree to Cléante's marriage to her. Cléante promises never to forget Jacques' kindness; Harpagon is on the point of tipping him, but changes his mind.

Father and son now thank each other for their reason-ableness—until each in due course finds out that Jacques has submitted incorrect messages to each. Once more they are quarreling bitterly—and Harpagon, threatening to disown his son, storms out.

La Flèche comes in with a casket under his arm. He has discovered Harpagon's buried treasure! Hearing the old man shouting, they run off. Harpagon comes in crying, "Thieves! Murderers!" He is beside himself. He will have the authorities find the robber. If necessary he will have the whole world hanged. "And if I don't get my money back, I will hang my-self!"

ACT V. Harpagon has engaged a magistrate, who boasts of the numbers he has helped hang for robbery. Whom does Harpagon suspect? Everybody. Harpagon wants him to arrest everyone in town and the suburbs. Jacques comes in, and is immediately accused by his master. Tactfully, the magistrate exonerates him and tries wheedling him into revealing what he knows of the robbery. In order to avenge himself on Valère for being such a favorite of the master, Jacques accuses him, and soon convinces Harpagon of Valère's guilt. Valère enters and is urged by Harpagon to confess to "the most horrible crime that was ever committed." The young man thinks he is referring to Valère's love for Élise, and admits he has done Harpagon an injury—but not a great one. After all, he continues, he is himself a man of rank, and he has done nothing that he cannot repair. He was spurred to act by a god who assures all his victims of being excused—the god of Love. HARPAGON: "The love for my gold pieces!" Valère denies that he has had any interest in Harpagon's wealth—as long as he is allowed to keep the treasure that he has got. He gets down on his knees to ask for the right to keep that treasure. Harpagon is sure that Valère is talking about the money, until Élise is mentioned. Valère cries that the servant Claude can bear witness to his whole conduct in the matter—and Harpagon thinks Claude an accessory to the robbery. When finally Harpagon understands that Valère is in love with his daughter, he believes him guilty of that crime and of the robbery too. Confused, not knowing of the robbery, Valère tries to justify his love—when Élise, Frosine, and Mariane come in. Harpagon vehemently scolds his daughter for being in love with a thief. Élise pleads for Valère as an upright man.

Anselme, whom Harpagon had destined his daughter to marry, enters, surprised at the emotional to-do. Harpagon explains that there is present one who dared ensnare Élise's heart. Anselme declares that for his own part he would never marry any woman against her will. Valère, charged anew by Harpagon, announces that all of Naples can bear testimony to his integrity. Anselme bids him be careful: he himself knows all of Naples. In that case, Valère stoutly maintains, Anselme must know Don Thomas d'Alburci. ANSELME: "No one knew him better than I." Valère introduces himself as Don Thomas' son. Anselme calls him a liar: it is at least sixteen years since that same Don Thomas perished at sea with his wife and children. Yes, Valère counters, but Don Thomas' son was saved from the wreck by a Spanish vessel. Lately learning that his father was not dead, Valère has been searching for him until, meeting Élise here, he became her slave and postponed his travels. He has a ruby seal of his father's and an agate bracelet of his mother's, as well as old Pedro, the servant, to fortify his story. Mariane cries out at this: Valère must be her brother, and her mother will be in transports of delight to see him. They too were saved, but by pirates, after which they were sold to slavery for ten years. Anselme realizes that she and Valère are *his* daughter and son; he is Don Thomas. Believing his own family dead, he was thinking of finding solace in a new marriage; he took the name of Anselme in order to forget his old sorrows. Hearing that Anselme is Valère's father, Harpagon demands of *him* the ten thousand crowns of which he has been robbed.

HARPAGON: This is your son?

ANSELME: Yes.

HARPAGON: I hold you responsible for paying me the ten thousand crowns that he stole from me.

ANSELME: *He* stole from you?

HARPAGON: He.

VALÈRE: Who told you so?

HARPAGON: Jacques.

VALÈRE: You're the one who said this?

MAÎTRE JACQUES: You see I'm saying nothing.

HARPAGON: Yes, you did. There's the Magistrate who has taken down his deposition.

VALÈRE: Can you believe me capable of so wicked an act?

HARPAGON: Capable or incapable, I want to see my money again.

Cléante and La Flèche enter. Cléante tells his father that if he will agree to the young man's marrying Mariane, the money will be returned. Anselme blesses the union, and counsels Harpagon that he will be well-advised to bless it too. Harpagon says that before he listens to any advice he wishes to see his money-box. He also adds that he has no intention of giving the young people any money when they marry; he is too poor for that. Anselme offers to defray the wedding costs. Harpagon makes him also promise to provide him with new clothes for the wedding. The Magistrate submits his bill for taking down all this testimony; Anselme agrees to pay for that too. While the others are rejoicing in their union and anticipating happiness, Harpagon can think of nothing but the joy of seeing his cash-box again.

TARTUFFE

The three-act version of *Tartuffe* had been presented only once, and then banned, chiefly through the machinations of a powerful secret religious organization, the Company of the Holy Sacrament, whose members were noblemen, attorneys, and certain members of the clergy. Though opposed by many of the hierarchy, including the Archbishop of Paris, the *"cabale des dévots,"* as it was called, continued to meet and to exert great influence; they were inveterate enemies of the stage.

They managed, through intermediaries, to procure the interest of the Archbishop of Paris and of the Queen-mother in suppressing *Tartuffe,* about which the *cabale* seems to have known even before it was performed.

Roullé's attack on Molière because of this play and its predecessors put him in the serious danger of having been publicly accused of impiety and a satirizer of religion. Knowing how false the charges were, Molière was most anxious to have his play seen by the Parisian public. To this end he appealed to the King to lift the ban on this work; but the King would not risk permitting a public performance as yet. However, private readings in the salons were allowed, as well as several private performances for the Duke of Orleans and the Prince of Condé. In the meantime Molière in his *Don Juan* replied to his enemies in that play's last act. From the King's continued patronage it is clear that he himself was sympathetic to his favorite dramatist, and in 1665 Louis bestowed upon Molière's troupe the title of The King's Company (*La Troupe du Roi*).

Hearing of *Tartuffe,* Christina, Queen of Sweden wrote to the French Secretary of Foreign Affairs for a copy of the comedy in 1666, but the latter answered that he was unable to oblige. At last Louis XIV authorized a performance in Paris, and the play was presented at the Palais Royal on August 5, 1667 with great success, under a new title, *The Impostor,* the hero's name being changed from Tartuffe to Panulphe, and certain passages being omitted. But Louis was off to his army in Flanders, and the man left in charge of the Paris police, who was himself a member of the *cabale,* forbade further performances. All of Molière's appeals proved fruitless. On August 11, 1667 the Archbishop of Paris expressly forbade everyone in his diocese to "present, read, or hear recited" *Tartuffe,* "whether publicly or privately, under whatever name . . . under pain of excommunication." This interdiction of course included Louis himself.

The Queen-mother died. In October of 1668 Louis came to terms with Pope Clement IX, and on Tuesday, February 5, 1669 Louis gave the royal permission to present the play in public. Four days later *Tartuffe,* in its five-act verse form as we now know it, was played, Molière himself enacting the role of Orgon.

No play has been more universally admired. Satire is at its most intense in this unmasking of a religious hypocrite; few characters in any play evoke more hatred from an audience than Tartuffe. Molière's dramatic skill is nowhere greater than here; he cunningly delays presenting his villain until the third act. We can hardly wait to meet the wretch, and yet we anticipate the encounter with dread and loathing. His deluded victim, Orgon, is depicted with biting satire too, but for him we have only pity. There is no mirth in the smiles this play evokes; we can be only bitter at the follies of human nature which the poet has so convincingly shown us. But even here, in the bitterest of his comedies, Molière never loses his basic sanity. The good sense of Orgon's brother-in-law, children, and wife reminds us throughout that humanity is not to be despaired of. The picture of their well-to-do middle-class life is beyond praise in its realism.

TARTUFFE

SCENE: *Orgon's house in Paris*

Persons of the Drama

Orgon: *husband to Elmire*
Damis: *his son*
Valère: *Mariane's lover*
Cléante: *Orgon's brother-in-law*
Tartuffe
Monsieur Loyal: *a sergeant*
A Police Officer
Elmire: *Orgon's wife*
Madame Pernelle: *Orgon's mother*
Mariane: *Orgon's daughter*
Dorine: *her maid*
Flipote: *Madame Pernelle's servant*

ACT I. At the opening we are introduced to Orgon's family. His second wife, Elmire, is much younger than he, and is deeply in love with him; she is on the best of terms with her two step-children, Mariane and Damis. But Orgon's mother, Madame Pernelle, whose head-strongness her son unfortunately inherits, does not at all approve of the household Elmire runs. She rebukes what she considers an extravagant and frivolous mode of life—such is her interpretation of the innocent amusements of her daughter-in-law. She alone seconds Orgon's new infatuation with Tartuffe; she informs her grandson that she will not listen to having that worthy man sneered at by a fool like Damis.

Orgon first came upon Tartuffe in a church, where the beggarly scoundrel was making a great display of his humbleness of spirit and piety. Orgon has insisted that his saint come to live with them; he arrived, as Dorine, Mariane's maid, puts it, "without a shoe to his foot," and now he has assumed the authority of master of the establishment. Shocked at their talk, Madame Pernelle leaves in a huff and threatens that it will be a long time before she sets foot in that house again.

Dorine gives Orgon's brother-in-law, Cléante, an account of Orgon's subjection to Tartuffe. He calls him "brother," and loves him a hundred times more than mother, wife, son, or daughter. He confides all his secrets to him, lets him direct all his action, is forever embracing him as though, for all the world, he were a mistress. He joys to see Tartuffe eat more than six others at table, and makes sure that he gets the choicest helpings. Tartuffe, skilled in duping Orgon, knows how to draw money from him at any hour. He criticizes the behavior of everyone in the family. Damis suspects that Tartuffe has influenced Orgon to oppose Mariane's marriage to Valère, both of whom love each other.

Orgon comes in, and asks for news of the family:

ORGON: How is everyone?

DORINE: The day before yesterday Madame had a fever all day and a terrible headache.

ORGON: And Tartuffe?

DORINE: Tartuffe? He's very well, robust and fat, with a healthy complexion and in the pink of condition.

ORGON: Poor fellow!

DORINE: At night she felt so sick that she couldn't touch her supper, so vicious was the pain still in her head.

ORGON: And Tartuffe?

DORINE: He ate by himself, while she was at table, and devoutly destroyed two partridges and half a hashed leg of mutton.

ORGON: Poor fellow!

DORINE: She didn't close her eyes a moment all night. Her fever kept her awake, and we had to sit up with her until morning.

ORGON: And Tartuffe?

DORINE: Agreeably overcome with sleep, he went from the table to his room, jumped into a nice warm bed, and with no effort at all slept until morning.

ORGON: Poor fellow!

DORINE: At length we convinced her that she ought to be bled. She was almost immediately relieved.

ORGON: And Tartuffe?

DORINE: He plucked up his courage anew, and, to strengthen himself, took four huge glasses of wine at breakfast to make up for the blood that Madame had lost.

ORGON: Poor fellow!

DORINE: Both of them, in short, are doing fine. And I'll tell Madame now how concerned you've been about her recovery.

Cléante is surprised that Orgon doesn't realize that Dorine was laughing at him to his face for his absurd devotion to Tartuffe. Ah, declares Orgon, if his brother-in-law really knew Tartuffe, and understood the great changes that saint has wrought in him! Why, "he has detached my soul from all friendships; and I could see brother, children, mother and wife die without caring a bit!" He disapproves of everything and has taken a particular interest in Orgon's wife—warning Orgon of everyone who looks too affectionately at her. His piety is incredible. He accuses himself of sin because of the veriest trifle; he is shocked by the smallest thing. Why, he blamed himself the other day for having killed a flea! Cléante warns him against those who are over-pious; he respects the truly devout—but they are the last to make a public spectacle of their piety. Orgon refuses to listen. To change the subject, Cléante brings up the matter of Mariane's marriage to Valère. Why is Orgon so evasive? Has he determined to break his promise to give her to Valère? But Cléante can get only the most mysterious of answers from his brother-in-law.

ACT II. Orgon is questioning his daughter about her feelings for Tartuffe. He cautions her: Let her watch out how she answers. SHE: "I'll say whatever you wish me to say." That he finds a sensible reply. Let her go on to say that she'd like Tartuffe for a husband. Shocked, she cannot speak such a falsehood. He is determined to make it a truth—when he notes that Dorine is eavesdropping on their conversation. Dorine now speaks up. She has heard of these new plans for Mariane, and has refused to believe them—not even from Orgon's lips. He must be jesting. She reminds him that Tartuffe is not only a bigot but a beggar too. Orgon defends his beloved saint by declaring that Tartuffe is a nobleman whose indifference to worldly matters has allowed his estates to slip through his hands. Dorine goes on lecturing him boldly, and he only gets angrier and angrier with her impudence. As for Mariane, her father tells her that he will not allow Valère to marry her because he has never seen him going to church. DORINE: "Do you expect him to run there at the hours you specify just so you can see him?" ORGON: No matter what they say, Mariane is to marry Tartuffe; they will live together "like two children, like two turtle-doves." He tries to browbeat Mariane into acceptance of his decree, but Dorine keeps interrupting him until he is exhausted, and must give up for the moment.

Dorine now scolds Mariane for not having opened her mouth in defiance of her father's outrageous design. But although Mariane dearly loves Valère, she admits being too much in awe of her father to speak up. What does she then propose to do? Dorine asks. MARIANE: "To kill myself." Dorine is out of patience with that sort of talk. Mariane asks how Dorine can expect her to exhibit her love for Valère before the world and behave like an undutiful child? Very well, then, counters Dorine, marry your Tartuffe. And she begins to paint the joys of being married to that wretch. That is enough to fill Mariane with panic, and she beseeches Dorine's aid. "No!" exclaims Dorine, "by my faith you shall be well Tartuffified!" But when the girl begins to weep, Dorine relents, and promises her that they will circumvent Orgon and Tartuffe.

Valère enters. He has heard that his sweetheart is to marry Tartuffe. He wants to learn her reaction to this new state of affairs.

VALÈRE: And what have you yourself decided, Madame?

MARIANE: I don't know.

VALÈRE: A polite reply. You don't know?

MARIANE: No.

VALÈRE: No?

MARIANE: What would you advise me to do?

VALÈRE: I'd advise you to marry him.

She is hurt at this irony of her wounded lover, and promises to take his advice. A lover's quarrel ensues, during which each promises to forget the other. Several times he is about to leave her forever, and each time returns on some pretext. After three such near-exits, he returns again:

VALÈRE: You see me for the last time.

MARIANE: Goodbye.

VALÈRE: (*He goes again; when he reaches the door, he turns back.*) Huh?

MARIANE: What is it?

VALÈRE: Didn't you call me?

MARIANE: You must be dreaming.

VALÈRE: Well then, I'll be going. Adieu, Madame.

MARIANE: Adieu, sir.

But Dorine has allowed this folly enough scope, drags back the not unwilling Valère, and, after considerable trouble, manages to join their hands with the wry observation, "You love each other better than you think."

Dorine advises them to pretend to comply with Orgon's nonsense. The important thing is to gain time. They must use the influence of everyone they can to bring her father back to the fulfilling of his promise to Valère. The lovers part, vowing eternal love to each other.

ACT III.   Damis is beside himself with annoyance at the situation in his father's house, and wants to deal directly with Tartuffe, to put him in his place. Dorine counsels leaving Tartuffe to Elmire, who seems to have some influence with him. Damis wishes to be present at the interview, but Dorine fears his hot temper and insists that he leave. But it is too late. Seeing Tartuffe approach, Damis hides himself in a closet.

Perceiving Dorine, Tartuffe speaks loudly to his servant Laurent, offstage, ordering him to put away Tartuffe's hair-shirt and scourge, and saying that he is on his way to distribute alms among the prisoners. He takes a handkercief out of his pocket and tells Dorine to cover her bosom with it: such sights encourage sinful thoughts. Dorine cannot understand his readiness to be tempted; she could see him naked from head to foot without being inflamed. Delivering her message that her mistress wishes to have a few words with him, she leaves.

Tartuffe is delighted at finding himself alone with Elmire, and says so. She tells him he must open his heart and be direct with her. He takes her hand and squeezes it hard, then places his hand on her knee. She pushes her chair back, but he draws closer. She tries to end his gallantries by coming to the matter in hand: is it true that Orgon wishes to marry Mariane to him? Tartuffe has heard something of this; but that is not the happiness he really looks forward to. She interperts his answer to mean that all his thoughts are fixed on Heaven. Suddenly, he begins to pour out his love for Elmire, with increasing passion. She reminds him that he is a pious man. But I'm nonetheless a man, he retorts. If his attraction to her be blameable, the fault is with her beauty. She need not fear that he will boast if she grants him her favors; unlike men at Court, he knows how to love discreetly; that is the advantage of loving anyone with his reputation—she may give him her love in safety. What if, she asks, I should tell my husband of your indecent proposals to me? He is sure she is too kind to do that. She promises to say nothing on condition that he encourage the marriage of Mariane to Valère.

Damis, who has heard all this, cannot bear it another minute, and pops out of the closet. He is determined to unmask Tartuffe to Orgon. Elmire tries to dissuade him: she wishes no scandal and feels she can accomplish more with tact. But the headstrong Damis will not suffer the plotting of this scoundrel any longer. He is delighted that his father approaches just in time.

In an outburst Damis reveals to Orgon how Tartuffe has just tried to dishonor him as a reward for all his tenderness to his saint. Elmire, upset, leaves. Orgon is amazed, and the hypocrite cries that he is indeed a wretched sinner, and there-

fore will deny none of the things alleged against him. Whatever shame they heap upon him, he confesses he deserves yet
more. Orgon turns on his son and chastizes him for trying
to tarnish the name of such a holy man with his falsehoods.
Tartuffe carries on his pretended sanctity: "Everybody thinks
me a man of God, but in truth I am worthless. Yes, my dear
boy, go on—call me treacherous, infamous, a lost wretch, a
thief, a murderer. . . . I shall not contradict you, I deserve
them . . ." Orgon cannot bear to see that good man humili-
ated and threatens to break his son's bones if he utters another
word. Tartuffe gets down on his knees, imploring Orgon
to spare his son. Orgon insists that Damis beg Tartuffe's forgiveness. When Damis refuses, his father declares him disin-
herited, and curses him in addition to that. He orders him
to leave the house forever.

Tartuffe, as the innocent cause of all this disturbance,
offers to leave the house himself. Orgon will not hear of it.
Tartuffe slyly suggests that Elmire could convince Orgon with
stories similar to those of Damis. Never! cries Orgon. Tartuffe
promises, in order to avoid false reports, to shun Elmire.
ORGON: "No. In spite of all of them, you shall be with her
all the time. . . . A faithful and honest friend, who is to be
my son-in-law, is dearer to me than son, wife, and parents."
He is also now determined to make Tartuffe his only heir,
and he will at once draw up the deed. Will Tartuffe accept
it? TARTUFFE: "Let the will of Heaven be done in everything."
ORGON: "Poor fellow!"

ACT IV. Cléante is blaming Tartuffe for allowing
Damis to be banished from his father's home. Even if Damis
has told a false story, Tartuffe ought to be Christian enough
to forgive the youth. Tartuffe disclaims any ill-feeling toward
the boy; nevertheless, if he comes back to the house, Tartuffe

will have to leave—otherwise gossips will say that Tartuffe knows himself to be guilty. How can Tartuffe justify his accepting all of Orgon's property, to which he has no right? TARTUFFE: "I intend [it] for the glory of Heaven and the well-being of my fellow men." Cléante presses the point: if Tartuffe cannot find it consonant with Heaven's wishes to live under the same roof with Damis, would it not be better for Tartuffe to depart? TARTUFFE: "Sir, it is three-thirty. My religious exercises call me upstairs. You will excuse me for leaving."

Dorine, Elmire, Mariane, and soon Orgon come in. Dorine begs Cléante's help in opposition to the marriage with Tartuffe. Mariane falls to her knees to beg her father to release her from obedience to his wishes in this instance; if he will not allow her to marry Valère, let him at least not force upon her a man she abhors. She is ready, in preference, to become a nun. Orgon retorts that the more repugnance she feels for Tartuffe, the better the marriage will be for her soul. He silences Dorine and Cléante when they wish to speak, and tells his wife that he knows she was part of the plot against Tartuffe; had not Damis been lying, she must have been more upset than Orgon found her. Elmire now offers to *show* Orgon that Damis has told the truth; he will then have to believe. Sure of Tartuffe's innocence, he agrees. The others are asked to leave, Dorine is sent to bid Tartuffe come downstairs, and Orgon is made to hide under the table. Elmire reminds him that she must be allowed to say anything necessary to make this hypocrite drop his mask. Let Orgon listen to as much as he needs to hear to become convinced. But let him not wait too long. . . .

Tartuffe comes in, half afraid that this is a trick. Elmire tells him that since her husband wishes them to be together at all times, she can now open her heart to him and listen—

all too readily, she confesses—to his passion. He is very wary. She goes further: the reason she tried to break off his match with Mariane was that she wanted his heart all to herself. Politely he thanks her; but may her tender words not originate in her desire to break off that match, rather than in her own interest in him? He will not believe her until he has experience to some of those favors which she now promises him. Coughing to warn her husband, Elmire tries to calm Tartuffe by saying that he is proceeding too rapidly. TARTUFFE: I think myself so little deserving of your favors that I "shall not believe anything, madam, until you have convinced my passion by some real proofs." She fences with him, making her excuse that adultery would offend Heaven. He answers that he knows the means of rectifying "the evil of the deed with the purity of our intentions." Elmire coughs louder. Orgon still does not emerge from under the table. Elmire in a panic cries that she must apparently grant Tartuffe everything "since people persist in driving" her to such lengths and are waiting for still more proofs of what she has said. Not knowing what to do, she asks her tormentor to open the door and see if her husband is anywhere in view. Tartuffe tells her not to worry about Orgon; "between ourselves, he is easily led by the nose." He goes out for a moment, and Elmire sarcastically asks Orgon why he doesn't wait until she has given herself to Tartuffe. The hypocrite comes back, arms extended to Elmire, crying that they are safe—when he sees Orgon. When poor Orgon pours out his disillusionment, Tartuffe would again try to make excuses, but is stopped and ordered out of the house at once. Suddenly the villain drops his mask, and retorts: "It's *you* who will get out, you who talk as though you owned it! This house belongs to *me!* I'll show you that I have . . . the means of . . . avenging offended Heaven, and of making those repent who speak of turning *me* out of this place!" He stalks off.

Elmire asks for the meaning of his words, and Orgon begins to tremble when he thinks of the deed of gift which he has drawn up in behalf of Tartuffe. He dashes upstairs to see whether a certain box is still there.

ACT V. Orgon is worried about the disappearance of the box. He tells Cléante that it was entrusted to him by a friend before he fled town; it contained papers upon which his friend's life and possessions depend. Orgon had told Tartuffe all about it and entrusted it to his keeping—so that, if questioned, he himself could deny having it. Cléante suggests that since Tartuffe now has the upper hand, Orgon ought to try diplomacy with him. But Orgon is through with all pious people henceforth. Cléante chides him for going from one extreme to the other; because this rascal has deceived Orgon, must one conclude that everyone is a hypocrite?

Damis comes in, ready to slice off Tartuffe's ears. He has heard the bad news and wishes to avenge his father's wrongs. Madame Pernelle, Elmire, Mariane, and Dorine enter. Orgon gives his mother a rapid sketch of Tartuffe's attempt to seduce Elmire and to reduce him to poverty by depriving him of his property. Dorine ironically appends: "Poor fellow!" Madame Pernelle refuses to believe her son's account, and considers it simple slander—even when he insists upon what he has seen with his own eyes. Appearances, she reminds him, are deceiving. She gets him into a boiling rage by her refusal to credit a syllable against that good man. Cléante interrupts their dissension: no time must be lost in taking steps against Tartuffe's machinations. Elmire cannot believe anyone could be so ungrateful as to carry out the threats Tartuffe has made; Cléante

knows that Tartuffe will do anything and moreover find pious
excuses for his knavery.

An Officer of the Guard comes in with a message from
Tartuffe. On Cléante's advice Orgon tries to speak mildly;
perhaps Tartuffe offers a reconciliation. The Officer, for all
his politeness, bears a summons which requires Orgon to quit
the house, bag and baggage, and make way for Tartuffe who
is now lord and master of Orgon's possessions, by virtue of
the deed of gift now in the Officer's hands. Damis is ready
to thrash the Officer, but Orgon manages to maintain a show
of calmness. Orgon will have until tomorrow morning to
leave; until then the Officer and his assistants will stay there
too, with the keys in their keeping. Madame Pernelle is at
last convinced of Tartuffe's true character, and Dorine mockingly blames Orgon for complaining against the hypocrite:
"His virtue is perfect in the love of his neighbor; knowing
that worldly possessions corrupt, he wishes out of pure charity
to take everything away from you which could interfere with
your salvation."

Valère enters. He has just been warned by a friend at
Court that Orgon must flee at once; Tartuffe has accused his
benefactor to the King of having kept the secrets of a state
criminal. A warrant is out for Orgon's arrest. Valère has his
coach waiting at the door to carry off Orgon; he himself
brings a thousand *louis d'or* for Orgon's use. He will go along
to make sure that Orgon will be safe. But Tartuffe comes in
with a Police Officer, and arrests Orgon in the King's name.

ORGON: You wretch! You've kept this blow for the last.
               This is the stroke, you villain, by which you
               are finishing me off. . . .

TARTUFFE: Your abuse cannot anger me. Heaven has
               taught me to bear all suffering.

The others turn on Tartuffe, and he asks the Police Officer to waste no more time and do his duty. The Police Officer is ready to comply—but it is Tartuffe whom he collars to go off to prison. The Police Officer explains: the King soon saw through Tartuffe's exterior to the vileness beneath. In betraying Orgon, Tartuffe betrayed himself—for information has long been accumulated against the hypocrite under another name. Volumes might be written detailing his crimes. The King annuls Orgon's deed of gift to Tartuffe, and pardons him for keeping in trust his friend's box of documents.

As Tartuffe is led off to jail, Orgon, in his senses at last, thinks with joy of celebrating the nuptials of Mariane and Valère.

MONSIEUR DE POURCEAUGNAC

During the hunting-season of 1669 Molière came to Chambord with the Court and was lodged there in wretched cold quarters for six weeks. He was coughing badly, and perhaps it was because he had need of the medicos that he again pilloried them in his new production of October 6, *Monsieur de Pourceaugnac,* a racy and rather grotesque farce in the form of a three-act prose comedy-ballet. Molière performed the title role, that of a bizarre member of the provincial gentry, and the composer Lully (who wrote the music) that of a doctor. M. Pourceaugnac, a doltish countryman from Limoges, arrives in Paris to marry Julie, who is actually in love with Éraste. With the help of Sbrigani, a sly Neapolitan, and Nérine, a woman of intrigue, the young lovers play an assortment of tricks upon poor Pourceaugnac, until he is very glad to leave Paris and go back to Limoges. The schemers, for instance, assure two physicians that Pourceaugnac is insane; after a consultation, the doctors employ apothecaries to administer the traditional cures—including that of the clysterpipe. At one point of the farce, the victim is pursued over the boards by a flock of apothecaries waving their enema-bags. The play, if coarse, is nonetheless very funny.

THE MAGNIFICENT LOVERS

At the beginning of 1670 the love-affair between Louis and Mme. de Montespan was at its height. As magnificent lovers themselves it was they who suggested to Molière the outline for his next piece, *The Magnificent Lovers,* which was a great success when produced at the château at Saint-Germain on February 4, 1670. Two suitors (Iphicrate and Timoclès) for the hand of a princess (Ériphile), rival each other in providing stunning entertainments for her. The entertainments were the ballets presented; the five-act play, in prose, shows how the princess cares for neither of her princely suitors, but is in love with and is loved by a general of lowly origins (Sostrate). A lucky chance falls his way: he is able to save the life of the princess' mother (Aristione), and as a reward can marry the girl he loves. The satire in this play is aimed at the astrologists.

THE WOULD-BE GENTLEMAN

On October 14, 1670 Molière presented at Chambord what has ever since been his most popular play, part prose, part verse, *The Would-Be Gentleman.* For the ballet-scenes Lully wrote some of his most charming music. The Turkish entertainment with which the piece concludes was very much in the mode; there was a new passion in Paris for everything Turkish.

From the elaborateness of, and the emphasis placed upon, the Turkish ballet, which had been commanded by the King, it is clear that with its first audience that was the center of interest. Yet *The Would-Be Gentleman* has often been performed in many countries (without Lully's music and with scant attention to the ballet) to the great delight of audiences, as a roaring farce. The play *is* excruciatingly funny. But it must always be something of a shock to anyone who has seen the comedy thus performed, to be present at its presentation at the *Comédie française* in Paris, where the traditions of Molière date from his own performances. Witnessed under those conditions, the comedy takes on a grace and charm, as well as a lightness, which would have seemed inconceivable to a mind accustomed to the play's coarser treatment. No doubt, the tone of the whole is rightfully set by Lully's enchanting music, and a production is doing best by the play by refraining from too broadly comic an interpretation. The hilarious lines are all the funnier when underplayed.

Molière never wrote a more completely original work. M. Jourdain, the role enacted by Molière, has become the type for the uneducated *parvenu*.

THE WOULD-BE GENTLEMAN

Le Bourgeois gentilhomme

SCENE: *A room in Jourdain's house in Paris*

Persons of the Drama

Monsieur Jourdain: *a bourgeois*
Madame Jourdain: *his wife*
Lucile: *their daughter*
Nicole: *a servant*
Cléonte: *Lucile's lover*
Covielle: *Cléonte's valet*
Dorante: *a count, Dorimène's lover*
Dorimène: *a marchioness*
Music Master
Pupil of the Music Master
Dancing Master
Fencing Master
Master of Philosophy
Master Tailor
Tailor's Apprentices
Two Lackeys
Singers, Dancers, Musicians, Cooks, the Mufti, Turks,
and Dervishes

ACT I. The overture is performed by a large collection of instruments, and as the curtain rises the pupil of the Music Master is seen alone at a table composing an air which M. Jourdain has requested in the form of a serenade. He hums the different parts to himself. The Music Master and the Dancing Master enter with their assistants. The Music Master explains that he set his pupil the task of composing the serenade while they have been waiting for Jourdain to wake up. Music and Dancing Masters congratulate themselves at having found so profitable a source of income as Jourdain—though it would be more agreeable if he could understand what they are doing. However, while others pay them with praise, he does so with coin of the realm.

Jourdain comes in, in dressing-gown and night-cap, attended by two lackeys. He had to keep the two Masters waiting because today he's dressing like a man of quality, and the silk stockings were so tight he thought he'd never get into them. He wants their opinion on his new suit and bids them examine the material of his dressing-gown. Then he removes his dressing-gown, which he hands to the lackeys, and exhibits his tight red breeches and green jacket. He is ready now for their artistic productions. He doesn't like the idea that the musical composition was left to a pupil, no matter how gifted. When the song is sung for him, Jourdain says that it's too dismal and made him sleepy. Couldn't they liven it up? He sings them a silly ditty to show the sort of thing that's really good. They compliment him on his voice, and urge him to study music himself. Very well, if that's what people of quality do. But the Lord knows when he'll find time, what with his lessons in fencing and philosophy. The music and dancing teachers urge upon him the greater usefulness of their branches of learning. The Music Master now presents a pastoral trio.

After it is sung the Dancing Master presents a suite of dances
—to provide the first Interlude.

ACT II. Jourdain approves the music and the dances.
There is to be a ballet for a lady who is doing him the honor
of dining with him. The Dancing Master leads him through
some dancing steps. Then Jourdain wishes to learn how to
bow properly to a marchioness. The Fencing Master is announced. He gives Jourdain a lesson. The Music Master ap-
plauds his performance. The Fencing Master belittles the
practices of dancing and music; the other two Masters, indignant, begin to quarrel with him. They are in the midst of a
scuffle when the Master of Philosophy enters. He tries to end
the squabble by quoting Seneca. When they explain what the
quarrel is about, he calls them impudent for daring to make
claims for their feeble studies in the presence of him, a philosopher. There is a free-for-all.

Finally Jourdain is left alone with the Master of Philosophy. He confesses to this teacher that above all he wishes to
become a scholar. They commence with the rudiments of
Logic, but Jourdain can't stand the sound of its vocabulary.
He doesn't wish Moral Philosophy nor Natural Science either.
What is the Master to teach him then? "Teach me to spell."
Then, later, "you can teach me the alamanac, so I'll know
whether there's a moon or not." The Master begins with the
vowels, giving Jourdain a precise description of how each is
pronounced. The long *e* sound, for instance, (*i,* in French) is
made thus: "Bring the jaws still nearer together and stretch
the corners of the mouth toward the ears." Jourdain is enchanted. Tomorrow they will take up the consonants—and
the Master gives him a few examples: how to pronounce D,
F, and R. Jourdain is so happy that he confides a secret to
his teacher: he's in love with a lady of quality and wants the

Master to help him write her a little note that he can drop at her feet. Does M. Jourdain want it in verse? "No, none of your verse for me." In prose, then? No, he doesn't want prose, either.

MASTER: But it must be one or the other.

JOURDAIN: Why?

MASTER: For the reason, sir, that to express oneself there is only prose or verse.

JOURDAIN: There's only prose or verse?

MASTER: That's all. All that isn't prose is verse; and all that isn't verse is prose.

JOURDAIN: And when one's talking—what's that?

MASTER: Prose.

JOURDAIN: What? When I say, 'Nicole, bring me my slippers, and give me my night-cap,'—that's prose?

MASTER: Yes, sir.

JOURDAIN: My goodness! For forty years I've been talking prose without knowing it!

In his letter he wants to say, "Dear Marchioness, your lovely eyes have made me die of love." The Master suggests some ornamentation. But all that troubles Jourdain with his note is whether he should put it the way he has just expressed it, or invert the same expressions in various ways.

The Master of Philosophy goes out, and the Tailor and his apprentice come in. Jourdain complains about the tight fit of his stockings and shoes. The Tailor has brought four boys to dress Jourdain in his new clothes, while they dance to the accompaniment of music. They flatter him by calling him, "My lord," as he tips them. He is entranced. The four tailor boys show their satisfaction by a dance with constitutes the second Interlude.

ACT III. Jourdain is going into town to show off his clothes. Nicole, the servant, almost dies of laughter to see her master tricked out in all his finery. He threatens her, she tries to contain herself, but it is more than she can manage. He warns her to get the house ready for the company he is expecting.

His wife comes in and takes him to task for his extravagant clothes. People will laugh their heads off at him. Is he learning to dance in preparation for the day when he'll be too feeble to walk? NICOLE: "Are you learning fencing because you intend killing someone?" MME. JOURDAIN: He'd spend his time more profitably if he looked about for a husband for his daughter. This last affair of hiring a Master of Philosophy is carrying his madness to extremes.

JOURDAIN: I'm ashamed of your ignorance. For example, do you know what you are speaking right now?

MME. JOURDAIN: Yes, I know what I am saying is well said. . . .

JOURDAIN: That's not what I'm talking about. I'm asking you what are those words which you are speaking?

MME. JOURDAIN: They're words of good sense, and your behavior isn't.

JOURDAIN: I'm not talking about that, I tell you. I ask you: that which I say to you, that which you have just said—what is it?

MME. JOURDAIN: Nonsense! . . .

JOURDAIN: It's prose, you ignoramus!

MME. JOURDAIN: Prose?

JOURDAIN: Yes, prose. All that's prose isn't verse, and all that isn't verse isn't prose. . . . Do you know how to sound a U?

Nicole complains about the way the Fencing Master dirties the floors with his great feet. Jourdain calls for the foils, hands one to Nicole, and gives her a lesson in fencing. She hits him several times. Mme. Jourdain says he has gone crazy from hanging around the gentry. She particularly has it against his newest friend from that rank. Jourdain defends his friend, a nobleman high in court: "He talks to the King just the way I'm talking to you." Mme. Jourdain has no doubt that this friend is borrowing her husband's money. JOURDAIN: "Isn't it a privilege to lend money to a man of that rank?" Jourdain sees this friend, Dorante, coming in.

Dorante loads Jourdain with compliments on his clothes; he was talking to the King about him only this morning. Dorante acknowledges Jourdain's great kindness in lending him money, and would like to settle with him.

JOURDAIN (*to Mme. Jourdain*): You see! What have you to say now, woman?

DORANTE: I'm a man who prefers to pay his debts as promptly as possible.

JOURDAIN (*to Mme. Jourdain*): Didn't I tell you?

DORANTE: Now, let's see, what do I owe you?

On Dorante's insistence, Jourdain tabulates the various loans.

JOURDAIN: "That adds up to . . . four hundred and eighty-three pounds." Dorante agrees. Then there were further sums, Jourdain reminds him, paid to Dorante's tailor, saddler, and other tradesmen, totaling one thousand seventy-five pounds.

DORANTE: Exactly. . . . Now, add to that another two hundred and twenty-five pounds which you're going to lend me, and that makes thirteen hundred pounds—which I'll pay you as soon as I can. . . .

MME. JOURDAIN (*to Jourdain*): This fellow's making a milk-cow out of you.

JOURDAIN (*to her*): Oh, do hold your tongue!

DORANTE: If it's inconvenient, I'll go somewhere else.

Jourdain protests that it's an honor to oblige him, and goes out to fetch the sum. In his absence, Dorante tries flattering Mme. Jourdain—to no avail. She answers him bluntly and without friendliness. Jourdain returns with the money.

Dorante now speaks of the Marchioness, who will appear soon to dine and see the ballet Jourdain will present in her honor; it was Dorante who persuaded her to come. Jourdain takes him to the side so that Mme. Jourdain cannot hear this talk. Dorante had the greatest difficulty in talking the Marchioness into accepting the diamond Jourdain sent her. Jourdain is grateful to him, and would go to any expense to open the lady's heart to him. Dorante says that Jourdain's serenades, flowers, firework displays, the diamond, and to-night's entertainment are bound to influence the Marchioness in his favor. Jourdain has arranged to get his wife out of the way by sending her to his sister's for dinner.

Annoyed at their private confabulation, Mme. Jourdain sends Nicole across the stage to overhear what she can. Jourdain catches her eavesdropping, gives her a slap, and leads Dorante out. Nicole is sure that something fishy is going on. Mme. Jourdain senses that her husband is involved in some love affair; she will get to the bottom of it. But first her concern is for their daughter Lucile; Cléonte loves the girl, and Mme. Jourdain would like to see it a match. Nicole is glad to hear this, for she is smitten with Covielle, Cléonte's valet, herself. Mme. Jourdain exits and soon Cléonte and his valet come in.

Cléonte and Covielle are both angry with Nicole—because, despite his devotion to Lucile, she has passed him by on the street as though he were a stranger. No doubt she has taken a fancy to Dorante. Cléonte asks Covielle to support him in his resentment by describing her in terms that will cause him to despise her:

COVIELLE: In the first place, her eyes are small.

CLÉONTE: That's true. She has small eyes. But they're full of fire, and bright, the most penetrating in the world, the tenderest.

COVIELLE: Her mouth is large.

CLÉONTE: Yes, but it has charms no other mouth has. It's a mouth that moves one to desires, the most attractive, the most loveable in the world.

COVIELLE: She isn't particularly tall.

CLÉONTE: No, but she's graceful and well-proportioned.

COVIELLE: She affects a nonchalance in speech and behavior.

CLÉONTE: True, but she's full of grace for all that, and her manners are irresistible . . .

This dialogue continues until it is obvious that Cléonte thinks her perfection.

Lucile comes in with Nicole. Cléonte elaborately ignores Lucile, and she asks whether their meeting this morning is the cause of his sullen air. She wishes to explain, but he will not listen. When she, in turn, becomes annoyed at his stubbornness, he begs her to speak to him. Finally, she relents and assures him that it was only because she and Nicole were in the company of her old aunt that she pretended to ignore him this morning; her aunt insists that a girl must shun the advances of all men. She is forgiven at once by Cléonte. Mme. Jourdain enters and urges Cléonte to ask her husband for Lucile's hand at once. Jourdain comes in, and Cléonte immediately speaks up for his beloved. Jourdain says that before he answers he has a question to put, "Are you a gentleman?"

Cléonte replies that he was born of honorable parentage, that he has served six years in the army with credit, and has enough money to maintain a good position in the world. But he cannot pretend to have a title.

JOURDAIN: That settles it, sir. My daughter's not for you.

CLÉONTE: What?

JOURDAIN: You're not a gentleman and you can't have my daughter.

MME. JOURDAIN: What are you trying to say, you and your gentleman? Are either of *us* descended from Saint Louis?

She reminds her husband that his father was a tradesman, just as hers was; their daughter would do better to marry a decent man of her own sort than a beggarly gentleman. JOURDAIN: "I've enough money for my daughter. All I need is rank. And I'm going to make her a Marchioness." Mme. Jourdain will never consent to her daughter's marrying above her station; she won't have a son-in-law who'll look down upon Lucile because of her background. She encourages Lucile to refuse such a marriage, and goes out with the girl, after her husband.

Covielle has a plan to take in Jourdain and at the same time help his master. They go out as Jourdain comes back, muttering, "I'd have given two fingers of my hand to have been born a count or a marquis!" A lackey announces Dorante and the Marchioness, Dorimène. Jourdain hastens to tend to last-minute arrangements.

The pair comes in, and Dorimène cannot understand why Dorante has brought her to a strange house. He replies that it is to avoid any scandal in their being seen together. She admits that her resistance to him is wearing thin because of his serenades, gifts, and the entertainment he has arranged for her today. (Obviously, Dorante has never mentioned Jourdain as the donor.) She is a widow, and she feels herself inclining more and more to the idea of marrying Dorante, as he has been pressing her to do. But she is distressed at all his expenditures on her. This diamond, for instance. He begs her not to speak of such trifles.

Jourdain comes in and finds himself too near Dorimène, after making two bows:

JOURDAIN: A little further off, Madame.

DORIMÈNE: What?

JOURDAIN: One step further, please.

DORIMÈNE: What then—?

JOURDAIN: Go back a bit for my third bow.

DORANTE: Madame, Monsieur Jourdain knows the manners of society.

JOURDAIN: Madame, it is to me a great enough glory to find myself so fortunate—to be so happy to have the happiness that you have had the kindness to accord me the grace to do me the honor of the favor of your presence. And if I had also the merit to merit a merit like yours, and which if the Heavens—envying my luck—had granted me—the advantage of finding myself worthy—of—

DORANTE: Monsieur Jourdain, enough. Madame's not fond of elaborate compliments. She knows you're a man of spirit. (*to Dorimène*) He's a decent fellow, but as you see a little silly in his manners.

Dorante warns him in a whisper to make no mention of the diamond he gave her. Jourdain is effusive in his thanks to both of them. Dinner is announced as served. Six cooks dance in, bringing on the table set with foods—to form the third Interlude.

ACT IV. They sit down to dinner, and Dorante manages to imply to Dorimène that this magnificent dinner was arranged by himself. Despite Dorante's warnings, Jourdain cannot resist referring to her lovely hands.

DORIMÈNE: No doubt you're referring to the diamond, which is truly beautiful.

JOURDAIN: Me, Madame? God forbid I talk like that. It would not be to act like a man of fashion. The diamond isn't much.

The singers sing two drinking songs. After them, Jourdain clumsily compliments Dorimène again.

DORIMÈNE: Goodness! Monsieur Jourdain is more of a gallant than I thought.

DORANTE: Indeed. What do you take Monsieur Jourdain for?

JOURDAIN: I could tell her what I'd like her to take me for.

Mme. Jourdain suddenly appears. So this is why he shipped her off to his sister's! There's a theatre downstairs and a feast fit for a wedding up here. This is the way he's spending his money! Dorante comes to the rescue by averring that it is he who is entertaining the lady; Jourdain is merely lending him the use of his house. Mme. Jourdain doesn't believe it and berates Dorante for taking advantage of her foolish husband and Dorimène for causing dissention in a respectable family by allowing Jourdain to think he's in love with her. Affronted, Dorimène leaves at once, followed by Dorante. Jourdain is so angry that he feels like throwing things at his wife.

Covielle enters, disguised as a traveler. He introduces himself as one who has known Jourdain since he was an infant; he was a close friend of Jourdain's father, a notable gentleman. This man knew Jourdain's father to be a *gentleman?* Without a doubt. Then why do the idiots insist that Jourdain Senior had been a tradesman? "Pure slander!" cries Covielle; he continues to relate that he has only just returned from his travels around the world. Does Jourdain know that the son of the Grand Turk is in town, with a fine retinue, and that he is being received in the great houses as a person of distinction? Good news for Jourdain—this young man has fallen in love with Lucile, and won't rest until he's Jourdain's son-in-law. Covielle adds realism to his story by throwing in some invented specimens of the Turkish language. In order that his father-in-law may be worthy of him, the Grand Turk's son wants to make Jourdain a "Mamamouchi"—according to Covielle—the greatest title of rank in Turkey. The young Prince is impatient for the marriage, and is therefore bringing to Jourdain's house everything needed for the ceremony of elevating Jourdain to Mamamouchi.

Cléonte comes in, wearing Turkish garb, three pages bearing his train. He talks gibberish which is supposed to be Turkish, and Covielle acts as his interpreter:

CLÉONTE: *Bel men.*

COVIELLE: He says that you must quickly go to prepare yourself for the ceremony, so that he can see your daughter after that, and conclude the marriage.

JOURDAIN: All those things in two words?

COVIELLE: Yes, the Turkish language is like that.

Jourdain follows Cléonte out. Dorante enters, and Covielle asks for his assistance in their little scheme.

The Turkish ceremony with dancing and music forms the fourth Interlude. Its pseudo-Turkish is a crazy mixture of authentic Turkish, Italian, Spanish, Egyptian, thinly disguised

French, etc. The ceremony involves Jourdain's getting down on his knees to act as a lectern, while the Koran is placed on his back, and the Mufti pretends to read from it; Jourdain is given a tuban and a sabre; during the dance, the dancers take turns hitting Jourdain with their scimitars. The ceremony ends with this bit of "Turkish":

> "*Non tener honta:*
> *Questa star l'ultima affronta.*"

(i.e., Don't be offended:/ The last affront is ended.)

ACT V.   Jourdain is practicing being a Mamamouchi as Mme. Jourdain comes in. He tells her she'll now have to be more respectful to a Mamamouchi like him. He repeats some of the Turkish ceremony, to her bewilderment. He goes out. Seeing Dorante and Dorimène approaching, she leaves.

Dorante entreats Dorimène's aid in Cléonte's behalf. There is still the ballet to be seen. Dorimène announces that the only way she can think of to stop Dorante's extravagances for her sake is to marry him. He is grateful. Enter Jourdain à la Mamamouchi. He salutes them with Oriental compliments: "Sir, I wish you the strength of serpents and the wisdom of lions . . . Madame, I wish your rose-bush may blossom all year."

Cléonte enters in Turkish costume, and Dorante pretends to pay his respects to his Turkish Highness. Lucile comes in. Jourdain tells her she must marry his Turkish Magnificence. She refuses—until she recognizes her lover underneath the disguise. Mme. Jourdain enters and is informed of the forth-coming marriage; she is astonished to hear that Lucile has agreed to it. She is obdurate, and threatens to strangle Lucile if she renounces Cléonte. Only after a to-do does Covielle manage to get her attention long enough to whisper to her the facts. She, of course, immediately consents too. To clear her mind of any further suspicions Dorante also announces his marriage to Dorimène. Jourdain concludes that Dorante says this only to throw Mme. Jourdain off the track.

While they are waiting for the Notary to draw up the marriage contracts, they all settle down to see the Ballet, which concludes the comedy.

PSYCHÉ

Molière's next work was another court spectacle, *Psyché,* written in collaboration, with Corneille and presented at the Tuileries in a room especially built for it, on January 17, 1671. This five-act tragedy-ballet, with music by Lully, employed some very elaborate machinery. A palace was made to vanish before the very eyes of the audience, and the gods made their entrances and exits flying through the air; there were clouds for a ballet on Olympus and scenery for Hades itself. The story comes from Apuleius. Psyché is so beautiful a girl that Vénus herself envies her. She orders her son (called alternately Amour and Cupidon) to inflame the maiden with the love for the ugliest of men. But Amour becomes enamored of Psyché himself and marries her; he conceals from her, however, his name and identity, and disappears every morning to return at night. Psyché's sisters (Auglaure and Cidippe), jealous of her, give her no peace about learning the truth concerning her mysterious husband. One night she gets up from bed and, lamp in hand, leans over sleeping Amour. A drop of burning oil falls on him; he wakes and flies away. Psyché is hurled into Hades, but at the prayers of Amour Vénus abates her enmity, and Psyché is placed in the ranks of the gods.

Because of the pressure of time, Molière composed only

the first act and a few of the later scenes. The play as a whole is not well put together, but it contains beautiful scenes, and these are still performed.

THE ROGUERIES OF SCAPIN

On May 24, 1671 Molière presented at the Palais Royal in Paris his delicious three-act prose farce, *The Rogueries of Scapin*. Scapin (from the Italian *Scapino*) was a traditional figure in the Italian *commedia dell'arte;* Molière himself played the role. The plot is largely an adaptation of the *Phormio* of Terence, but Molière has converted the stock figure of Latin comedy into a clever scamp of a valet. A great deal of the story is recollective of the *commedia dell'arte,* yet the dialogue could have been penned only by Molière. The comedy was highly praised by Bayle and Voltaire, but Boileau wrote that he could not recognize the Molière he admired in all this buffoonery.

THE ROGUERIES OF SCAPIN

Les Fourberies de Scapin

SCENE: *Naples*

Persons of the Drama

Argante: *father to Octave and Zerbinette*
Géronte: *father to Léandre and Hyacinthe*
Octave: *Argante's son, and Hyacinthe's lover*
Léandre: *Géronte's son, and Zerbinette's lover*
Hyacinthe: *Géronte's daughter, and Octave's lover*
Zerbinette: *Léandre's lover*
Scapin: *Léandre's valet, a rogue*
Sylvestre: *Octave's valet*
Nérine: *Hyacinthe's nurse*
Carle: *a rogue*

ACT I. Octave has been informed by his valet Sylvestre that his father, Argante, is arriving this very morning—bad news because Argante is returning home with the express intention of marrying Octave to Géronte's daughter, who is being sent over, for the purpose, from Taranto. Octave foresees reproaches from his father for what he has been up to, and Sylvestre expects more than reproaches for himself.

The rascally Scapin, valet to Léandre, Géronte's son, comes in. Scapin offers to help; he reminds them that he has had a reputation unparalleled in the fine art of scheming. Of course, after a recent brush with the law, he has more or less decided to turn over a new leaf and "do no more for anyone." Octave tells how, when two months ago Argante and Géronte went off on a business trip, they left their sons in care of their respective valets, Sylvestre and Scapin; soon thereafter Scapin's master, Léandre, fell in love with a gypsy girl.

One day the sounds of weeping led Octave to the bedside of an old woman who was dying, with a beautiful girl attending to her. Her tenderness to her dying mother moved the people who crowded into the house, to tears; "anyone would have fallen in love with her." Octave has been thinking of no one else since, but after the old woman's death the servant has forbidden him the house, unless he was prepared to marry the girl. After endless self-torture, Octave married her three days ago; since he hasn't a penny, she is living in direst poverty. To make matters worse, Argante is returning two months before expected, prepared to marry Octave to Géronte's daughter (by Géronte's second marriage at Taranto). Scapin considers that the case is not so hopeless, and adds: "I wish I'd had the opportunity to lead those old fellows by the nose when I was in my youth!"

Hyacinthe, Octave's beloved, comes in weeping. She has heard of his father's return and fears it may alter his love for her, especially since he is dependent on Argante. Her lover assures her that he would renounce everything in the world for her. Scapin is impressed with the girl's beauty and good sense, and he encourages the lovers to seek his aid, so that he can break his oath to meddle no more in the affairs of others.

Hyacinthe goes out, and Scapin rehearses with Octave how the boy is to speak to his father, Scapin speaking the lines of an angered Argante. In the middle of this Octave sees his father approaching and he runs off in terror.

Argante is muttering to himself about his son's marriage, about which he has already been informed. Scapin is very cordial with him, and Sylvestre maintains a terrified silence. Scapin tries to diminish the gravity of what Octave has done; he himself has already lectured the boy but in the end was convinced that Octave has only fulfilled his destiny. Didn't Argante sow his wild oats when *he* was a lad? Wasn't *he* more than fond of the ladies? And here's Léandre who has done something far worse than Octave. Well, Octave was enchanted with his girl, wooed her—but was surprised by her kinsmen and obliged to promise marriage. The alternative was to be killed by them; would Argante prefer to have his son dead? Argante decides, on hearing this version, that there are good grounds to have the marriage dissolved. Scapin tells him that Octave will never cooperate. Argante cries that he'll disinherit his son if he's stubborn. SCAPIN: "You'll never have the heart to do it . . . You're far too kind." ARGANTE: "I'm not the least bit kind—I can be as mean as anyone else when I choose to!" As Argante goes out, he laments that Octave is his only child; why could not have Heaven spared him his daughter?

Scapin tells Sylvestre that he needs him now for a trick that must be played; Sylvestre will have to disguise himself as a blackguard. Who cares if this will mean three years in the galleys to both of them?

ACT II. Géronte and Argante are deploring Octave's marriage, but Argante will soon put an end to that. GÉRONTE: "If you'd brought up your son the right way, he'd never have played the trick upon you." ARGANTE: "I suppose you've brought up your son better?" Knowing nothing precise, Argante hints that Léandre has done something even worse than Octave—as Scapin has told him—and goes off to see a lawyer. What can possibly be worse, Géronte wonders, than marrying without a father's consent?

Léandre comes in and tries to embrace his father, but is prevented. Géronte first wants to know what his son has done; Léandre insists upon his guiltlessness. GÉRONTE: "Scapin has told me the truth . . . You traitor! If it's true that you've dishonored me I'll disinherit you!" Géronte exits angrily. Léandre is resolved to avenge himself on Scapin.

Octave comes in with Scapin, whom he is thanking for his aid. Léandre tries to beat his valet, but Octave intercedes. Léandre demands a full confession from his valet, now on his knees: Scapin admits to having shared a cask of his master's wine with some friends; then he admits to other pranks. Léandre promises to settle with him for those later; what he wants now is to know what Scapin told his father. Scapin swears he hasn't even seen Géronte.

A bravo enters to tell Léandre that some gypsies are about to carry off Léandre's sweetheart, Zerbinette. She implores him to bring money within two hours or he will lose her forever. Léandre now begs for Scapin's help. The latter gets up and crows over his master's sudden humbleness, and forces him to apologize for his late threats. He at length softens and agrees to assist. Léandre and Octave both need money; Scapin resolves to get it from their fathers. He dismisses both young men, seeing Argante approaching.

Scapin advises the old man against starting any law-suit; it can only mean terrible complications for him. Scapin has a better way: he has already seen Carle, the brother of Octave's girl, a ruffian, convinced him of how easy it would be to dissolve the marriage, and got him to agree to settle the thing out of court for a sum of money. But Argante balks at the huge sum, even though Scapin assures him he has talked the brother into vastly reducing his original demand, and warns that a law-suit might cost more. Sylvestre comes in disguised as the ruffian-brother; he announces that if Argante goes on with the law-suit he will cut him up in ribbons. Argante hides behind Scapin in terror. When the ruffian notes the presence of Argante, Scapin introduces him as not Argante, but as Argante's deadly enemy. The ruffian shakes Argante's hand rudely and exclaims: "I give you my word . . . that I'll dispatch that wretch for you before the day is over!" Then he gives a display of his swordsmanship, and exits. Argante is convinced; he will agree to the money. He is at first reluctant to trust Scapin with it, and the latter feigns to be offended and to wash his hands of the whole business. He lets himself be coaxed into accepting it.

Argante goes out and in a minute Géronte comes in. Pretending not to see him, Scapin begins to wail aloud over Géronte's unhappy lot. Géronte wishes to know what is wrong, and Scapin tells him. He was trying to console Léandre for his father's rough treatment, as they walked along the road at the harbor. A courteous Turk invited them aboard a handsome Turkish galley, where they supped magnificently. While they were feasting the galley slipped out to sea. Afterwards Scapin was thrown into a skiff and told that unless he brought back the ransom, Léandre would be shipped off to Algeria. Géronte, too, is loath to part with the money demanded, scolds Scapin for ever getting into the galley, and suggests that Scapin return and offer himself as an exchange for Léandre until the sum can be scraped together. But, Scapin reminds him, they'd never accept a poor wretch like himself as a substitute. After a great deal of hesitation, the valet gets Géronte to part with the money. Géronte goes out cursing. Scapin is gleeful, but is not through with the old man yet. He will be avenged for his lying about him to Léandre.

Octave and Léandre come in. After teasing them, Scapin hands over the money they need.

ACT III. The gypsy-girl Zerbinette and Octave's Hyacinthe come in under the guidance of Sylvestre and Scapin. Zerbinette is not sure of Léandre's intentions; she is grateful for being ransomed, but he is not to assume any rights over her because of that. More than money will be required for her to return his passion: i.e., marriage. Scapin assures her that that is what his master plans, but she fears his father's interference. Hyacinthe says that she and Zerbinette have had similar adventures, fears, and misfortunes; that should make them friends. But Zerbinette reminds her that Hyacinthe at least knows who her parents are and can hope to find them again; she herself has nothing like those high hopes to anticipate. Scapin will help them resolve their troubles: he enjoys risks. They all go and leave him alone.

Géronte comes in. Scapin tells him his son is now safe, but there is new danger. Some people are looking for Géronte to kill him. Octave's brother-in-law thinks that Géronte wants to have the marriage dissolved so that Octave can marry Géronte's daughter, and that ruffians are searching for Géronte everywhere. To help save him Scapin tells him he must get into a sack and not budge. Scapin will carry the sack and get the old man home. There they can barricade themselves and call for assistance. (Scapin in an aside tells us that this will be his revenge against Géronte for lying about him to Léandre.)

Géronte gets into the sack. Scapin assumes a foreign accent and by changes of voice pretends he is several different desperadoes looking for Géronte. When Scapin, in his own voice, speaks up in Géronte's defense, the imaginary ruffians beat him—and the sack. Scapin cries out as though he had been soundly whacked. The ruffians are made to say farewell, and Géronte puts his head out of the bag, unable to muffle his pain any more. He begins to upbraid Scapin, when the latter sees another member of the gang approaching, and Géronte has to hide again. This desperado thinks he sees something moving in the sack, but Scapin bravely will not let him look into it. More beatings. Géronte's head appears, then quickly ducks in again as several new voices are heard. While Scapin is having a fine time, Géronte peeps out again and sees what is happening. He gets out of the sack. Scapin sees him and runs away.

Zerbinette comes in laughing. At Géronte's demand to know the cause of her laughter, she tells him it is a funny story she's just heard about a trick a young man played to get money out of his father. She tells him, not knowing who he is, how this father, one Géronte, was defrauded of his money by the conniving of the servant Scapin. In a rage, the old man goes out, threatening punishment for them all.

Sylvestre comes in and informs her that the man she was just talking to was Géronte, Léandre's father. Hearing his master call, Sylvestre pushes Zerbinette off. Argante comes on and accuses his servant of plotting with Scapin to deceive him. Sylvestre protests his innocence. Géronte enters; they compare notes on how they have been cheated of money. Géronte adds worse news: today, when he expected to greet his daughter on her arrival from Taranto, he learns that she left there a very long time ago, and it looks as though she had perished at sea.

Nérine, his daughter's nurse, enters and flings herself at

his feet. She has been looking for him under the name he bore at Taranto, Pandolphe. He asks for his daughter, and she tells him he will soon see her; but first Nérine begs forgiveness for having allowed the girl to marry a youth named Octave, son of Argante. Astounded at the coincidence, Géronte goes to meet his daughter.

Scapin comes in, and is told that Octave's affairs are happily settled. But the two old men are out for Scapin's scalp. He'd better watch out; the two sons may make peace with their fathers at Scapin's expense. Seeing the others approach, Scapin leaves.

Géronte, Argante, Hyacinthe, Zerbinette, and Nérine come in. Octave joins them. Octave learns that he has unwittingly married the girl destined for him. They are all supremely happy. Hyacinthe wants Zerbinette welcomed too; but Géronte is unwilling to play host to the girl who insulted him. Léandre enters. His father need worry no more about the girl he intends to marry. The people who ransomed her have revealed that they stole her from a good family right here in Naples when she was four; they have also given him a bracelet she then wore and by which her family may be traced. Argante recognizes the bracelet as that of his long-lost daughter.

A desperado comes in to tell all that a mason's hammer fell on Scapin's head as he was passing a building; he's dying now and wishes to make his peace with Géronte and Argante. Scapin is carried in by two men, his head swathed in bandages. He implores forgiveness for what he has done so that he may die in peace. They both forgive him. He begins to feel better because of their forgiveness. GÉRONTE: "But I forgive you only on the condition that you die." Argante, however begs his old friend not to ruin the general happiness, and forgive Scapin unconditionally. Géronte yields.

THE COUNTESS D'ESCARBAGNAS

Another court spectacle, *The Countess D'Escarbagnas,* was presented at Saint Germain on December 2, 1671 on the occasion of the second marriage of the King's brother to the Princess Palatine. In this comedy of provincial manners, Molière satirized the financiers of his day through the person of M. Harpin (his name was deliberately recollective of Harpagon's). This little piece shows how the Countess, a provincial woman of rank, ignorant and gauche, after a trip to Paris affects the manners of Paris in her native Angoulême. Her simple servants cannot make head or tale of her preciosity. Among the brilliantly-drawn satirical portraits are those of her son's tutor, the pedantic Bobinet; the stupid pretender to learning, Tibaudier, the lawyer; and Harpin, the brutish tax-collector. It has often been lamented that Molière never saw fit to make a full-length comedy out of this excellent material.

THE LEARNED LADIES

In 1669, the year of *The Miser,* Molière confided to Donneau de Visé his intention of writing a more perfect play than any he had written heretofore. This piece, of which he could well be proud, was *The Learned Ladies,* a five-act comedy in verse, presented for the first time in Paris on March 11, 1672. Molière performed the role of Chrysale. It was a great hit with the public.

The Learned Ladies is an extension and a deepening of the satire of *The Ridiculous Precious Ladies;* after thirteen years the attack on preciosity is renewed, but the field of ridicule is broadened to include feminine education. These affected women are also pretenders to learning—with a strong bent toward philosophy and the sciences—and begin to feel the equals of men, if not their superiors. This play has often been imitated by other dramatists, and in England a number of comedies were later adapted from it. The satire is of the kind that can never be dated.

THE LEARNED LADIES

Les Femmes savantes

SCENE: *Chrysale's house in Paris*

Persons of the Drama

Chrysale: *a good bourgeois*
Philaminte: *his wife*
Armande ⎱
Henriette ⎰ *their daughters*
Ariste: *Chrysale's brother*
Bélise: *Chrysale's sister*
Clitandre: *Henriette's lover*
Trissotin: *a wit*
Vadius: *a philosopher*
Martine: *a kitchen-maid*
L'Épine: *a lackey*
Julien: *Vladius' valet*
A Notary

ACT I. Armande, the elder, and Henriette, the younger,
daughter of the wealthy bourgeois, Chrysale and his wife
Philaminte, are talking. Armande is shocked that Henriette
can be so vulgar as to think of getting married. The word

"marriage" is enough to make her shudder with the dreadful images it evokes. For her part, Henriette cannot imagine anything more desirable than to have a good life with a husband who returns her love. Armande bids her rise above such mundane hopes and devote herself to things of the mind. Their mother, for example, is everywhere honored for learning; why will not Henriette be a worthy daughter to such a woman? Henriette believes that not everyone is cut out for philosophy; let everyone follow his own bent. How lucky for Armande that their mother was subject to the weaknesses Armande complains of—else where would that sister-scholar be? Well, sighs Armande, let us at least hope that you're not thinking of Clitandre as a husband. Why not? asks her sister. Well, replies Armande, everyone knows he has courted *me*. But without result, Henriette reminds her; your thoughts are placed on higher things than marriage; since you don't want him, why shouldn't I? Because, her sister answers, it is always pleasant to have an admirer; besides, knowing I've rejected him, can you be secure in the love he now offers you? Well, rejoins Henriette, here he comes; let him enlighten us as to the facts.

Henriette demands that Clitandre speak the truth; Armande pretends that she wishes to spare him the embarrassment. But he has no objections to the truth, and tells it. He did love Armande sincerely, but was treated by her with such contempt that he sought someone more humane. He found such a girl in Henriette. He is enslaved to her and doesn't want to be released. But Armande warns both that her sister's first duty is to obey whatever plans her parents may make for her marriage. She goes out in a huff.

Clitandre wishes to speak at once to Henriette's father, but she assures him that it is more important to win over her mother: her father is too gentle a soul to try to rule the house.

Clitandre shies away from this: he is no admirer of learned women, and hence is never at ease with Philaminte. Her favorite, Trissotin, bores and irritates him, despite Philaminte's vast admiration for Trissotin's intellect and auctorial abilities. Henriette agrees with her lover's estimate; nevertheless, he *must* procure her mother's approval. This, Clitandre knows, will mean praising the writings of Trissotin, which he despises.

Seeing Bélise, Chrysale's sister, approaching, Clitandre asks his beloved to leave him alone with her. He begins to broach his love for Henriette, but the girl's aunt thinks he is speaking of his love for herself. She halts him at once. She has enrolled him among her lovers, but he is to be consumed with passion without letting her know it. He corrects her at once: he is talking of his love for Henriette. She decides that he is being merely tactful, and is in genteel fashion referring to her under Henriette's name—as a "figure of speech." Despite his protests to the contrary, he cannot get her to see that it is not with her that he is in love.

ACT II.   Ariste, Chrysale's brother, has promised to help Clitandre. Before Ariste can broach the matter of Clitandre's love to Chrysale, Bélise comes in. She hears Ariste tell of Clitandre's passion for Henriette. Bélise assures them that the young man's love is for someone else: none other than herself. Her brothers are astonished that anyone is in love with her. Offended, she rattles off a list of her other admirers: Dorante, Damis, Cléonte, Lycidas.

ARISTE: These people love you?

BÉLISE: Yes, with all their might.

ARISTE: They've told you so?

BÉLISE: None of them has taken the liberty. . . .

ARISTE: Damis hardly ever comes to the house.

BÉLISE: That's to show me a more submissive respect.

ARISTE: Dorante insults you everywhere with stinging
           words.

BÉLISE: Those are transports of a jealous rage.

ARISTE: Cléonte and Lycidas have both taken wives.

BÉLISE: That's because of the despair to which I've re-
           duced their ardor.

Ariste declares his sister a victim of self-deluding fancies; she
exits haughtily. Chrysale thinks she is daft. Returning to the
matter of Henriette's lover, Chrysale is only too pleased to consent to Clitandre as a son-in-law, even though the youth has
no great fortune. Ariste suggests getting Philaminte to agree
too. Pretending to more authority than he has, Chrysale
pronounces that unnecessary: Ariste can consider the arrange-
ment settled. Ariste leaves.

Martine, the kitchen-maid, comes in. Philaminte has just
discharged her; Chrysale wants her to stay. Philaminte comes
in with Bélise; she is angered to see that Martine hasn't yet
quitted the premises. Chrysale wishes to know what the wench
has done wrong. Without explaining, Philaminte turns on her
husband for not supporting her wishes. Before he knows it, he
too is telling Martine to go, without knowing why. Perhaps
Martine has broken a mirror or a piece of porcelain? Nothing
so trivial! Has she been found stealing something? No!

PHILAMINTE: "She has with unheard-of insolence, and after
thirty lessons, shocked me with the impropriety of a barbarous
and low word, which Vaugelas the grammarian specifically
condemns." Philaminte would like to see her husband condone
such a crime. Bélise adds: "She destroys all sentence-structure,
though she's been taught the laws of language a hundred
times." Martine feels she is doing well enough with her speech
if she can make herself understood. Her ungrammatical self-
defense is intolerable to the ears of these ladies, and poor
Chrysale is forced to tell the girl to go.

When she has left he defends her. What difference does her offense against grammar make if she does her work well in the kitchen? His wife scores him for his materialism. She and Bélise begin to criticize adversely his old-fashioned vocabulary. He has had enough, and reads them a lecture. A mother ought to be concerned over the manners and morals of her children and to manage the household, instead of interesting herself in life on the moon. His servants, in order to please his wife, all have scientific aspirations, and neglect everything else. The one poor girl who was not poisoned by all this intellectualism has just been turned out because of her grammar. His wife and sister are horrified at his vulgarity of mind.

Bélise having left, Chrysale broaches the subject of Henriette's marriage. Philaminte has decided that Monsieur Trissotin, whom Chrysale despises so much, would be the best husband for their daughter. There's no point in arguing, she informs him, and the matter is settled, so far as she is concerned. He is not to say anything yet to Henriette. She leaves.

Ariste comes in and learns from his brother of Philaminte's choice of Trissotin for Henriette. Ariste is exasperated that Chrysale has said nothing of Clitandre. How can his brother be so weak? It's all very well for Ariste to speak, his brother replies, but he has no idea of the degree to which quarrels upset Chrysale. Philaminte has a terrible temper. But he loves her just the same. ARISTE: "You let yourself be dragged around by the nose like a fool . . . Resolve, once and for all, to be a man . . . Will you shamelessly allow your daughter to be offered up to the foolish fancies which your family is afflicted with? Will you endow an idiot with all your riches because of the six words in Latin which he spouts?" Chrysale is shamed into admitting this; his cowardice must end. He asks Ariste to send for Clitandre, and announces: "I've put up with it too long. In spite of everyone I'm going to be a man."

ACT III. Philaminte, Armande, Bélise, and Trissotin are gathered to hear some of Trissotin's verses, the lackey (L'Épine) being in attendance. In the most affected way the women lavish praises upon Trissotin before he reads a line. Henriette comes in, but seeing the nature of the gathering, tries quickly to withdraw. She is forced to stay. L'Épine is scolded for tripping over a chair: he should know better, having been taught the law of equilibrium.

The ladies urge Trissotin to hasten to furnish the intellectual repast they are all waiting for. TRISSOTIN: "To feed this great hunger exhibited before me, a single dish of eight lines seems to me little enough, and I think I should not do ill to add to the epigram—or, rather, to the madrigal—the spice of a sonnet which at the home of a princess was thought to have some delicacy." As Trissotin starts to read, Bélise keeps interrupting him with exclamations of how her heart is beating violently in anticipation of hearing him.

He reads "a sonnet to the Princess Uranie on her fever." It is a wretchedly affected and pedantic affair. The enraptured ladies vie with each other in murmuring to themselves the striking phrases; they are moved to ecstasy:

BÉLISE: Ah, gently, I beg of you. Give me time to breathe!

ARMANDE: Please give us the leisure to admire.

PHILAMINTE: These lines make one feel, to the depth of one's soul, I-don't-know-what that brings one close to swooning.

They clamor for a repetition of the remarkable second stanza. At the conclusion of the third:

PHILAMINTE: One cannot bear any more!

BÉLISE: One swoons.

ARMANDE: One dies of pleasure.

Having heard not a word from Henriette, Trissotin asks whether his lines have been annoying her. HENRIETTE: "Not at all. I'm not listening."

Trissotin recites his epigram, *Upon a Coach Colored Amaranth, Given to a Female Friend*. This, too, is greeted with effusion. Philaminte is pleased that he appreciates the female intellect. Women, she declares, are capable of all the demands of science and language. Pseudo-intellectual talk follows. Trissotin is fond of Aristotle, Philaminte of Plato, Armande of Epicurus, and Bélise of the atomic system—though she finds "a vacuum hard to accept." Philaminte has seen men on the moon, Bélise has seen steeples there. Armande states that they will study "grammar, history, poetry, ethics, politics, as well as physics" thoroughly. They will purify the language of all its commonness. ARMANDE: "Because of our laws we shall judge literature. Because of our laws, everything in prose and verse will be submitted to us. No one will have any taste except us and our friends. We shall seek everywhere for something to chide, and we shall discover that no one knows how to write well but us."

L'Épine announces the arrival of Vadius, a learned man who has pressed Trissotin for an introduction to Chrysale's family. According to Trissotin, Vadius knows all the ancient authors, and is a great Greek scholar. The ladies (except Henriette) are again enthralled, and allow themselves to be embraced by the newcomer. Trissotin and Vadius vie with each other in flattering the works of each other. Their praise gets more and more fulsome—until Trissotin asks his friend whether he's ever heard the little sonnet on the Princess' fever? VADIUS: "Yes, and it's worthless; if you had heard it, you'd agree with me." When Trissotin reveals himself to have been its author, Vadius apologizes: he must not have given it his full attention while it was being recited. He wishes to read his own ballad; Trissotin speaks slightingly of the ballad form. Soon the two are vilifying each other as dunce, petty scribbler, cad, etc. Each defends himself on the grounds that he has been worthy of an attack by the great Boileau. In anger Vadius leaves.

Philaminte tells Henriette that she is tired of having her daughter a disgrace to this learned family. To cure her obtuseness, Henriette is ordered to look upon Trissotin as a husband. Bélise thinks her niece is reluctant to accept his heart because it already belongs to Bélise, but she surrenders Trissotin to Henriette. Trissotin is delighted at Philaminte's words. The girl begs him not to conclude that anything has been arranged. Henriette offers him to her sister Armande; but, though she'd be glad to accept him if she wished a husband, Armande is a foe to matrimony. The other women have left.

Chrysale brings Clitandre in and tells Henriette that she is to marry the young man. Henriette is only too anxious to obey him. Armande protests that it is her mother's wishes which must be hearkened to. Chrysale silences Armande. Ariste is proud of his brother, and Clitandre is overjoyed.

ACT IV. Armande reports to her mother what her father has done, and how rapidly Henriette has acceded. Philaminte promises to put an end to Clitandre's hopes: knowing she wrote, Clitandre has never asked her to read him any of her compositions! Clitandre enters, at first unseen and unheard. Armande fans the flames of Philaminte's resentment by saying that in the old days, when Clitandre was courting *her*, he never esteemed her mother. When she read some of Philaminte's verses, he did not like them. Clitandre steps in to ask for "a little honesty." What wrong has he ever done Armande that she so much wishes to destroy him? Her answer is: his infidelity to his first love. How is he unfaithful? he asks. He gave his heart once entirely to her, but she rejected it. Is it not she who is to blame that he now loves her sister? Why, she asks him, was he not noble enough to keep his soul above the need of the senses, and cherish her intellectually? He admits sadly to having a body as well as a soul; he is incapable of her pure loftiness. After all, if he is vulgar because he approves of marriage and all that goes with it, he is no worse than most of the world . . . . Well, then, she says, although he is so coarse, she agrees, since he is unequal to rarified celestial love, to marry him. CLITANDRE: "You're too late, madame." He will not wound the girl he now loves as repayment for her goodness to him when he was in misery over Armande's refusal of his love. Philaminte interrupts: her consent to any marriage in this family is needed, and she has chosen another mate for Henriette. Clitandre deems it an insult to have a fool like Trissotin for a rival.

Trissotin comes in, and some heated words follow between him and Clitandre on the subject of learning, the latter being of the opinion that learning can make some people into fools; the more he has seen of such men, the more charming ignorance seems to him. Trissotin explains Clitandre's defense of ignorance as a product of the young man's having been at Court, and Clitandre defends the Court as the residence of good taste and sound judgment; he also speaks scornfully of those who delude themselves into thinking that if their writings are printed they thereby become important to the state.

Julien, Vadius' valet, arrives with a note from his master to Philaminte. It warns her against allowing Trissotin to marry Henriette; he wishes to do so only because of the family's money. Vadius is going to write a satire against Trissotin; in the meantime he sends Philaminte Horace, Virgil, Terence, and Catullus, with marginal annotations to show where Trissotin has plagiarized the ancients. Philaminte declares that this new abuse of her favorite had only determined her to hasten the marriage; indeed, it will take place this very evening. Armande tells Clitandre that she is sorry that his desires must be contravened; Clitandre vows to deprive her of that sorrow.

The valet, Philamante, Trissotin, and Armande have gone out. Chrysale, Ariste, and Henriette come in. Clitandre beseeches the help of Chrysale to prevent the marriage of Henriette to Trissotin this evening. Chrysale, his brother being present, sounds very firm in his intention to give his daughter to Clitandre. Henriette urges her uncle to keep Chrysale in this mood. She promises Clitandre that if she cannot be his, she will enter a convent.

ACT V. Henriette tells Trissotin that, being a philosopher, he ought to rise above wishing to marry her because she has money. He protests that he loves her only for her beauty. She confides to him her love of Clitandre and is firm in her inability to love Trissotin. He is sure he can teach her to love him; besides, what is he to do, since he does love her— would she not first have to lose her charms before he could be cured of his affection? Why should he want her when he has so many other admirers? Henriette asks. Ah, he loves them only as a poet, is his answer; her, he loves as a man. He goes out, still determined to be her husband.

Chrysale, Clitandre, and Martine enter. Chrysale has given Martine her job back; he is going to teach his wife the duties of a married woman. Henriette hopes his firmness will survive the day. He is so very stern about his rights as head of the house that he begins to make one worry about his stand.

Philaminte, Bélise, Armande, Trissotin, and a Notary come in. Philaminte asks whether the Notary could not revise his usual barbarous style and draw up a document more literary. She wants the sums of the dowry to be translated into coins of the ancient world (minae and talents instead of francs) and the date into ides and calends. Philaminte is angered at seeing Martine in the house; her husband says that they will discuss that matter later.

When the Notary is filling in the names, Philaminte indicates as the groom Trissotin, Chrysale, Clitandre. The poor Notary is at sea, not knowing whom to obey. Philaminte turns upon her husband; Chrysale defends himself, and is backed by Martine, who says that the man ought to give the orders. She goes further and states the superiority of Clitandre over Trissotin as a prospective husband. Listening impatiently, Philaminte ends by re-affirming her position; if Chrysale has given his word, let Clitandre marry Armande instead of Henriette. Chrysale weakly asks the young man whether that wouldn't be a good solution. Bélise reflects out loud that there *is* a solution which would please him more; but his love for her must remain immaterial, "pure as the morning star."

Ariste enters as the bearer, he says, of two pieces of unfortunate news. One is in the form of a letter from Philaminte's notary: because of her neglect of her affairs, she has lost a law-suit which she ought to have won; she must pay forty thousand crowns in expenses. The other is a letter to Chrysale telling him that the money he has entrusted to two men is gone, for both went bankrupt. Chrysale has lost all he possesses. His wife is ashamed of his making a fuss about it; no true philosopher would. Besides, Trissotin's wealth will suffice for all of them. But Trissotin begs out: since everyone opposes the marriage, he withdraws.

At long last Philaminte sees him for the knave he is. Pretending affront at the way he has been treated, he leaves at once. Clitandre, however, has not altered his desire to marry Henriette despite the family's sudden impoverishment, and

Philaminte is touched; she is only too glad now to agree. But Henriette loves him too much to wish to burden him with their misfortunes, and she now objects to a marriage.

Is that her only reason for resisting Clitandre? asks Ariste. Well, then, let her cheer up. The tidings he has brought were false, a trick to force his sister-in-law to see what Trissotin really is like. Their fortune is unimpaired. Everyone rejoices at this revelation. There are no further impediments to the union of the lovers. When Armande protests, Philaminte tells her to fall back on philosophy for consolation. As for Bélise, she can only hope that Clitandre is not marrying Henriette out of frustration and despair over his unrequited passion for the girl's aunt.

THE IMAGINARY INVALID

Molière's last play, *The Imaginary Invalid,* was produced at the Palais Royal on February 10, 1673. It is likely that he had hoped to exhibit this three-act prose comedy "mixed with music and dance" at the Court before this, but was prevented from doing so because of his quarrel with the composer Lully. A first-rate musician, Lully was extraordinarily vain and ambitious, and a very great favorite of Louis XIV. In March of 1672 the King gave him the right to establish the Royal Academy of Music in Paris (the origin of the present *Opéra* in that city), and this grant made Lully the monopolist of music in the capital. Soon no theatre other than that composer's was permitted to have more than a specified limited number of singers and instrumentalists; and none of these could be those in Lully's employ. His dancers were also not allowed to appear elsewhere.

Now, Molière had habitually presented lavishly conceived

ballets at Court, and was thus severely handicapped in any future productions. Moreover, with Louis' permission to produce and publish all the songs and ballets for which he had written the music, Lully in November 1672 presented *The Feasts of Cupid and Bacchus,* a ballet consisting almost entirely of passages from Molière's plays. Molière therefore collaborated with the composer Charpentier for his last work. But Lully's monopoly caused the diminution of the ballet's magnificence to the degree that it was considered not lavish enough for Court presentation.

Molière had already attacked the doctors in *Don Juan, L'Amour médecin, Le Médecin malgré lui,* and *Monsieur de Pourceaugnac.* In this play he assembled all that was most devastating as well as most comic of medical absurdities—not only of the profession but of traditional medicine itself. Having had need of medical help himself, Molière knew only too well the uselessness of the physicians with their antiquated dependence upon purgatives and bleeding—for no matter what sicknesses, as well as their obstinate deafness to new theory or discovery. The play, and particularly the final ballet, go further than he had ever gone in the causticity of his attack. Perhaps the most satirical passage he ever wrote against the medicos is this ballet, which ridicules the rites involved in the granting of a doctor's degree. As outrageous as it seems, it was not so far from the fact, however. When the Faculty of Paris awarded the degrees, the hall was decorated as in this play; the chairman-medico made an address eulogizing the Faculty and the profession; the doctor-to-be presented his thesis and had to answer questions; later the entire Faculty entered the hall with great pomp; the candidate had to take an oath to adhere to the Faculty's laws, another to attend the meetings, and a third to oppose all pretenders to the profession; another examination followed; the academic hat was placed on the candidate's head;

then the new doctor made an address in ornate Latin, expressing to all his gratitude.

Himself in the gravest ill-health, and further embittered by Louis' abandoning him in favor of Lully, Molière, it is the more remarkable to consider, for this great comedy was able to summon (for what he may very well have felt would be his final work) his most brilliant energies. The play was very successful. A week after its première, while enacting the role of the Invalid, Argan, on Friday, February 17, Molière suddenly found it difficult to pronounce the word *Juro* ("I swear") during the Third Interlude. He managed somehow or other to continue to the end. At the conclusion of the piece, he was hurried home and went to bed. He coughed up a stream of blood, and died an hour later.

THE IMAGINARY INVALID

Le Malade imaginaire

SCENE: *A room in Argan's house in Paris*

Persons of the Drama

Argan: *the imaginary invalid*
Béline: *his second wife*
Angélique: *his daughter, and Cléante's lover*
Louison: *Argan's younger daughter, Angélique's sister*
Béralde: *Argan's brother*
Cléante: *Angélique's lover*
Monsieur Diafoirus: *physician*
Thomas Diafoirus: *his son, and nephew to Purgon*
Monsieur Purgon: *Argan's doctor, and uncle to Thomas Diafoirus*
Monsieur Fleurant: *Argan's apothecary*
Monsieur Bonnefoy: *a notary*
Toinette: *Argan's servant*

[Prologue. Set in "a charming country scene," this pastoral prologue celebrates the return of Louis XIV from his victories in Holland. The characters are the goddess Flore (Flora), the god Pan, nymphs, shepherds, and shepherdesses; the entire piece was sung, with intermittent dances, and hymned Louis as a conqueror.

The Alternate Prologue, much shorter, consists of the plaint of a shepherdess that all the skills of the doctors cannot cure her of the pangs of love. This little prologue was written to replace the first, probably because later the victories were not those of the French.]

ACT I. Argan, the imaginary invalid, alone in his room, is seated behind a table, computing his health bills with counters, and talking to himself. In most instances he finds the charges too high and decides to pay his apothecary only a portion of what he has been billed. It is obvious, from his recitation of the drugs and injections listed, that Argan's life is made up of one dosage or cure after another, the livelong day. This month he has had eight lots of medicine and twelve injections; last month he took twelve lots of medicine and twenty injections. "I'm not surprised that I don't feel as well this month as I did the last!" He rings petulantly for his servant, Toinette, and shows no patience until she puts her head in at the door. He wants to know whether, as a result of his injection, he has passed much bile today. TOINETTE: "Let Mr. Fleurant [the apothecary] stick his nose into that. That's his business." He gives orders for the hot water for the next injection, which is due shortly, and asks to have his daughter Angélique sent in.

Angélique enters and her father has hardly begun to speak to her when he must answer a call of nature, and hurries out. Angélique wants to talk to Toinette on her favorite topic, her young man, Cléante. He is all perfection; Toinette teases her about him and the seriousness of his intentions. However, the servant ends by admitting his declaration yesterday that he was going to ask for her hand would seem to indicate that he is not a flirt.

Argan comes back and informs his daughter that he has had a proposal of marriage for her. Sure that it is Cléante he means, she is very happy; she assures Argan that if he wants her to be wed, it is her duty to obey. Her stepmother, he tells her, has set her heart on sending Angélique and her little sister Louison to a convent, but Argan has given his word to his daughter's suitor and will keep it. Angélique and her father take turns in praising the prospective bridegroom—until Argan says the young man is to take his doctor's degree in three days. Angélique is astonished. But in a minute it becomes clear that Argan has not been talking of Cléante but of Thomas Diafoirus, sons of Doctor Diafoirus and nephew of Argan's own doctor, Monsieur Purgon. The marriage was arranged this morning, and the young man is to be brought over to meet Argan. Toinette rebukes him for wishing to marry his daughter, with all the money he has, to a doctor; she demands to hear his reasons. He replies: Because I'm in such poor health, I want to marry her into the medical profession so I can have all the help I need within the family. Toinette retorts that since Angélique is not ill, she has no need of a doctor and ought to marry to please herself; he'd better give up the idea—Angélique will never agree to it. Argan points out that Thomas will be heir not only to his father but to his uncle as well—and Mr. Purgon has eight thousand a year! TOINETTE: "He must have killed off plenty of patients to have made all that money!" A lively argument ensues between irritable master and saucy servant. He threatens to ship his daughter off to a convent if she's rebellious; Toinette scoffs at the idea—Argan is too kind to do a thing like that. Finally:

ARGAN: I absolutely order her to get ready to marry the man I say.

TOINETTE: And I absolutely forbid her to do it.

He is in such a rage that he chases Toinette with a stick around the chair, but she easily eludes him. He is compelled to pause for breath; his daughter and Toinette run out.

Béline, his second wife, comes in. He tearfully complains to her of Toinette's impudence; he has asked her often to discharge the girl. Béline reminds him that all servants have faults: this one is capable and hard-working.

Béline calls in Toinette and asks her why she was annoying Argan. The artful servant says that all she did was to agree that, although the match with Dr. Diafoirus' son was a good one, it would be better to put the girl in a convent. Béline finds nothing wrong with such common sense.

She arranges the chair comfortably with pillows for her whimpering spouse, pulls his night-cap down over his ears to protect him from the draught, and fusses over him. Toinette drops a pillow on his head—to keep the dew off him—and runs off, as he throws the pillows after her. He is so upset that it will take eight doses of medicine and a dozen injections to set him to rights again. Béline sympathizes with him. She is, he declares, his only consolation.

ARGAN: To try to show some appreciation of the love you have for me, I want, my darling, as I told you, to make a will.

BÉLINE: Ah, beloved, let's not talk of that, I beg you. I can't bear the thought of it. The very word 'will' makes me tremble with misery.

ARGAN: I told you to speak of it to your notary.

BÉLINE: He's in there. I brought him with me.

Bonnefoy, the notary, is summoned—as Béline continues to protest her inability to discuss such matters. The notary is aware of Argan's wishes, which she has already communicated. But he tells Argan that it will be impossible in Paris that a husband provide by will for his wife. He continues: "The only provision man and wife can make each other is by a mutual gift while they're still alive—and at that, there must be no children of either or of both of them at the time of the decease of the first to die." There are, of course, various ways to get around the law—and the notary enumerates them. Béline protests anew her sensibilities' wounding at such talk; life would not be worth living if Argan should die.

BÉLINE: I shall follow you to the grave to show you my tenderness.

ARGAN: Beloved, you're breaking my heart. Take comfort, I beg you.

NOTARY: These tears are unseasonable. Things haven't gone that far yet.

Argan's only regret is that he has no child by her; Purgon promised him to enable him to beget one. In the meantime, he will have to follow the notary's directions; but to make sure, he's going to hand over to Béline twenty thousand gold francs and also two promissory notes due to him.

BÉLINE: No, no, I'll have nothing to do with this. How much did you say . . .?

ARGAN: Twenty thousand francs, my love.

BÉLINE: I beg you not to talk any more about money! How much are those two notes for?

ARGAN: My love, one is for four thousand francs and the other for six.

They go off to Argan's study to draw up the will, Béline tenderly taking every care of her "poor boy."

Toinette and Angélique enter. Toinette knows that Béline is up to some mischief against the girl's interests; Angélique doesn't care what her father does with his money as long as he will let her marry Cléante. Toinette knows she can help her: Béline is forever trying to get the servant as an ally, but Toinette cannot bear her. In order to help Angélique, however, Toinette will have to pretend to fall in with Béline's aims; she will have her lover, Polichinelle [Punchinello], the old usurer, make Cléante acquainted with Argan's plan to wed his daughter to the doctor's son.

[FIRST INTERLUDE. scene: *A street*. Polichinelle has come to serenade his sweetheart at night. He is interrupted first by the musicians and then by the dancers. He laments the power of love. Because of this she-dragon he adores, he suffers torments. He takes up his lute and sings his love, begging for her pity. On old woman appears at the window, ridicules him, and sings her disparagement of love. He is further interrupted by some violinists, and then by a group of archers. The archers seize him: he has these alternatives—he will give them money for drinks or he must suffer twelve slaps on his rump or twenty tweaks of his nose. He chooses the last. He gets beaten on the behind too. He finally gives in, and hands them some money. They all dance out their good-nights.]

ACT II. Cléante has come to learn Angélique's feelings about the marriage her father would arrange for her. He has come as the friend of her music master, who has authorized him to say that he is to take the music master's place today. Toinette tells him to withdraw a moment. Argan enters. Purgon told him to walk up and down his room in the morning, twelve times each way, but forgot to state whether it should be lengthwise or across the room. Cléante is introduced, and makes the error of expressing satisfaction at Argan's apparently feeling better. Toinette pretends to take offense: better? Her master has never been worse. Argan sadly agrees.

Angélique is called to meet her substitute music-teacher. She manages to let him know that she thinks of him constantly.

Toinette comes back to announce the arrival of the Diafoiruses, father and son. The son turns out to be a great booby, clumsy and tactless. He approaches Argan as his father-in-law-to-be in a highly platitudinous and pedantic style. His father approves of his speech. Argan tells Angélique to greet Thomas.

THOMAS: Am I supposed to kiss her?

DOCTOR: Yes, yes.

THOMAS: Madame, it is with justice that the Heavens have yielded you the name of mother-in-law, since—

ARGAN: That's not my wife, it's my daughter you're talking to.

THOMAS: Where is she then?

ARGAN: She's going to come.

THOMAS: Shall I wait, father, till she's here?

DOCTOR: Pay your compliments to the young lady.

He makes her an equally stuffy harangue. Argan compliments the doctor on his son. Diafoirus agrees that he has reason to be proud: Thomas has neither imagination nor wit—and that is a good sign in a doctor; he never played games as a child; he was nine before he learned the alphabet—but that sluggishness was symptomatic of a sound judgment to come; at school he had to work harder than the others; he has made a name for himself at the Faculty for his unrelenting disputations; best of all is his attachment to the opinions of the ancient authorities in medicine, and his utter rejection of the idea of the circulation of the blood. Thomas draws a great roll from his pocket, a thesis against the circulation of the blood—a gift for Angélique. One of these days he is going to invite her to come and witness a dissection of a woman. Diafoirus is planning for his son a practice, not at Court, but among the general public. The trouble with people at Court is that "when they're sick they absolutely demand getting cured."

Argan suggests to Cléante that Angélique sing for the company. Cléante is willing; he hands her a paper on which he says her part has been written. What they are going to sing is a kind of rhythmical prose, such as two people might use speaking together. He outlines the situation of the little opera: A certain shepherd sees a boorish fellow behaving insolently toward a shepherdess; he chastizes the bully, goes toward the shepherdess, and falls in love with her; all he wishes is to serve her for the rest of his life; but he is not able to see her again, because she is kept under lock and key; he decides to ask for her hand in marriage, but learns that her father has just arranged to marry her to another; with the desperation of love, he finds means to get into her father's house to learn her feelings; there he meets his unworthy rival; the sight fills him with rage; but her father's presence prevents her from speaking to him except with her eyes.

Cléante and Angélique now sing a duet in which she expresses her loathing of her father's choice and her love for the "shepherd"; she will die rather than marry the other man.

Argan interrupts the little opera. He doesn't approve of it at all. He asks to look over the words, and finds that none of them have been written down; he sees nothing on the papers but the notes. Cléante explains that the newest method is "to write notes and words in one." Cléante is dismissed by an annoyed Argan.

Béline enters and meets Thomas. He begins again the harangue intended for her. Argan asks Angélique to give Thomas her hand; but she pleads for more time. Béline feels that there is a better solution than marriage for Angélique.

The girl speaks out clearly for her own rights to marry and to choose her husband herself. Argan thunders: either Angélique marries Thomas within four days or into a convent she goes. The girl leaves; so does Béline.

Before the Diafoiruses go, Argan asks them to see how he is. Diafoirus tells his son to take Argan's pulse. Thomas finds the pulse strong, then weak, then erratic. Argan is very ill; he has the symptoms of "a disturbed splenetic parenchyma." Argan observes that Purgon finds it is his liver which is bad. Of course, murmurs Diafoirus, spleen and liver are intimately connected. ARGAN: "Tell me. How many grains of salt ought I take with an egg?" DIAFOIRUS: "Six, eight, ten, etc. Always even numbers. With pills you always take odd numbers." The two medicos soon leave.

On her way out of the house, Béline slips in again to warn Argan that she saw a young man momentarily with Angélique. Little Louison was there, too; she'll be able to tell him all. As Béline goes out, the child comes in.

Argan asks her whether she hasn't seen anything today. The child answers, No. He is about to hit her with his cane when she admits that her sister told her not to reveal what she saw. Argan threatens her anew with the whip, and she pretends to be dead. He gets into a panic and begins to cry over her. The child comforts him: she isn't dead yet. He now questions her narrowly, and learns that the substitute music-master came back to see her sister. What did he say? "He told her this and that, that he loved her very much, and that she was the most beautiful person in the whole world." Then he went down on his knees and kissed her hands. Then Béline came to the door and he ran away.

Argan's brother, Béralde, enters. He has come with an offer of marriage for Angélique. Argan doesn't wish even to hear about it. His brother says that he has brought along some gypsies in Moorish dress to dance and sing for them. It will be as good for Argan as one of Purgon's prescriptions.

[SECOND INTERLUDE: Four Moorish girls sing songs hymning the *Carpe diem* philosophy. When love comes your way, take it. Dancers enter with monkeys; they dance with the Moorish girls and make the monkeys perform.]

ACT III. Béralde is talking with his brother, but Argan has to run out again to answer a call of Nature. Toinette begs Béralde to help the lovers. She adds: "I've been thinking that it would be a good idea ·to introduce into this house a doctor of our own to make him sick of Purgon and ridicule his methods. And, if we can't find anyone ready to do that, I've decided to indulge a fancy of my own." She runs out on seeing Argan returning.

Béralde wants to know why his brother is talking of putting Angélique into a convent; he sees the wicked hand of Béline in this. Or why does he want to marry his daughter to a doctor's son? Because, says Argan, that's the sort of son-in-law he has use for. Perhaps, says Béralde sarcastically, when little Louison grows up Argan will marry her to an apothecary? ARGAN: "Why not?" Béralde explodes: no one has better health than Argan; he must have a constitution of iron, seeing that he has been unable to ruin it will all the medicines he has been taking. ARGAN: Purgon says that if he absented himself from Argon's house for three days Argan couldn't survive. Doesn't Béralde believe in medicine at all? No, he looks upon it as "one of mankind's greatest follies"; he knows no more ridiculous piece of mummery, nothing more absurd, than for one man to assert that he can cure another: too little is known about the human organism as yet; the art of doctors is a mixture of high-sounding nonsense—words instead of accomplishment, promises instead of results. Medicos like Purgon will "send you into the next world with the best of intentions, and in murdering you do no more than they would do for their own wives or children, or, if necessary, themselves." What would Béralde propose doing when he is ill? Nothing but rest; Nature will cure him. "Most men die not of their diseases but their medicines." Argan counters: In other words, "all the world's knowledge is contained in *your* head."

BÉRALDE: I could have wished to have taken you, both to draw you a little out of your errors and to divert you, to see one of the comedies of Molière on this topic.

ARGAN: This Molière of yours is quite intolerable with his comedies. He finds it awfully amusing to make fun of decent people like the doctors!

BÉRALDE: It's not at all the doctors he makes fun of, but the absurdities of medicine. . . .

ARGAN: The devil, you say! If I were a doctor I'd get even with him for his impudence. When he's ill I'd let him die without help.

Béralde tries to change the subject and bring it back to Angélique But Fleurant, the apothecary, comes in with a syringe in hand. Argan excuses himself to Béralde: it's time for his next injection. His brother asks him to put it off to another time, so they can enjoy a little peace. Fleurant is indignant at Béralde's interference. BÉRALDE: "Go away, sir. It's obvious you're not used to speaking to people's *faces*." Fleurant is furious, and will tell Purgon, Argan's physician, of this tampering with doctor's orders. Purgon enters in a rage. He has heard that Argan is rebelling against his doctor! He gives Argan a tongue-lashing for daring to have refused

the injection, and then and there he casts his patient off forever. He also tears up the marriage settlement he had drawn
up in favor of Thomas, his nephew. Argan pleads to be taken
back as a patient, and insists that it was all his brother's fault.
It's of no use. Purgon prophesies a terrible end for Argan: "I
abandon you to your wretched constitution, to the disorder of
your bowels, to the corruption of your blood, to the bitterness
of your bile and to the dregs of your humors . . . I hope that
before four days you'll be in an incurable state. . . . That you
will fall into bradypepsia, from bradypepsia into dyspepsia,
from dyspepsia into apepsia, from apepsia into lientery, from
lientery into dysentery, from dysentery into dropsy, and from
dropsy to the loss of life to which your folly will have led
you." Argan begs for mercy, to no avail. Doctor and apothecary leave in anger. ARGAN: "Oh, my God! I'm dead. Brother,
you've done for me. . . . I'm at the end of my resources. I
feel already that medicine is avenging itself."

Toinette enters, saying that a new doctor is asking to
see Argan; strange to tell, this medico and she look as alike
as two peas. Argan is delighted that he has a medico to replace Purgon, and is eager to see him. Toinette, disguised as
this doctor, comes in; then begs to be excused a moment;
Toinette comes in as herself; then goes out and returns as
the doctor once more. He is a traveling physician, and soon
finds from Argan's symptoms that Purgon and others have
been wrong; it's neither Argan's liver nor spleen which is in
trouble, but his lungs. This doctor is shocked at the diet prescribed for the patient, and orders a heavy rich one with
plenty of wine. Everything is going well until the doctor
decides that Argan had better have one arm off and an eye
out. The doctor takes his leave to be present at a consultation—
over the body of a man who died yesterday. Argan is less

than pleased with this physician. He doesn't like the idea of losing an arm and an eye.

Toinette comes back as herself. Béralde speaks up for Cléante again, but now Argan is firm in his intention of sending Angélique to a convent. Béralde remarks that this decision will please Béline, and is disgusted at his brother's gullibility. Toinette pretends to defend Argan's wife: Béline loves her husband beyond measure. Would Béralde like to see the proof of her affection? Béline is about to appear: let Argan lie down as if dead, and Béralde hide in the closet—they will soon hear the utter devotion of this woman. Argan is pleased at the ruse, and slumps in the chair as if dead.

Béline enters while Toinette is giving loud vent to her grief.

TOINETTE: Your husband is dead.

BÉLINE: My husband is dead? . . . You're certain?

TOINETTE: Certain. . . .

BÉLINE: Heaven be praised! At last I'm relieved of a great burden. What a fool you are, Toinette, to afflict yourself over his death. . . . Who's going to feel the loss? Of what use was he? A trouble to everybody, dirty, disgusting, with his eternal injections or doses of medicine in his belly, forever blowing his nose, coughing, spitting—witless, boring, bad-tempered. . . .

Béline wishes to delay spreading the news of Argan's death until she has got hold of his keys, his papers and his money. Argan wakes up from his mortal sleep: "So, my lady, that's how you love me!" Béline runs out.

Toinette sees Angélique coming in, and asks Argan to put her to the same test. Enjoying the game, Argan dies again. Angélique is devastated by the news of her father's death. She

is inconsolable at the thought that he should have died angry
with her.

Cléante comes in, overwhelmed at what he learns. Angélique tells him that there can be no more talk of marriage
between them; she must go to a convent, as her father desired.

Argan arises, delighted with his daughter. Béralde joins
his entreaty to hers and Cléante's for the marriage of the girl
to her beloved. Moved, Argan declares: "Let him become a
doctor and I'll consent." Cléante is only too willing, but
Béralde has a better idea. Why doesn't Argan become a doctor himself? All he needs is the cap and gown of the profession, and the rest will come of itself. Toinette joins in the
persuasion. Seeing his brother charmed by the notion, Béralde
announces that the ceremony of induction into the profession
can be performed here and now, right in Argan's house. Argan
hastens out to make himself ready. And Béralde justifies the
forthcoming nonsense on the grounds that they are going
along with Argan's fancies—besides, it's Carnival time.

[THIRD INTERLUDE: The ceremony of Argan's induction is conducted in a mixture of Latin, Italian, and French
—a jumble intended to ridicule the Latin of the medicos.]
EXAMPLE:

> *Non possum, docti Confreri,*
> *En moi satis admirari*
> *Qualis bona inventio*
> *Est medici professio . . .*

("I cannot, learned colleagues, wonder enough at how fine
an invention the medical profession is.") The ceremony involves eight attendants with syringes, six apothecaries, twenty-
two doctors, and Argan attended by eight surgeons. There is
much pomp, music, and dancing. After a hymn to the pro-

fession, one doctor asks the illustrious company the reason for opium's causing one to sleep. Argan answers: because opium contains a soporific quality. The answer is correct. Other medical questions are propounded. He answers with the same profundity. Argan is at last asked whether he will abide by the laws of the Faculty? He answers: "I swear." (*Juro*) He takes a similar oath to abide by the opinions of the ancients, good or bad. Argan finally is given the doctor's hat and is declared a physician. He delivers his acceptance oration.

Molière died on February 17, 1673, at the very height of his creative powers. As an actor he was thereby excommunicated from the Church; his enemies had also seen to it that his reputation as a writer of impious plays was kept alive. Consequently, as he lay on his death-bed, two priests of the parish refused to attend him or administer the last sacraments. A third was finally persuaded to come, but by the time he arrived Molière was dead. Since he had died without the last rites of the Church, permission was at first not granted to bury him in sanctified ground; but, after friends petitioned, this harshness was revoked, and he was buried in the cemetery of St. Joseph's. Only a handful of mourners was present.

MOLIÈRE AS A GREAT COMIC GENIUS

The French do not hesitate to place Molière even above Shakespeare as the world's greatest writer of comedy. It is true that he lacks Shakespeare's wealth of poetic imagination and endless variety. But on almost every other ground he has no superior. The boundless sanity of Molière is matched only by his unfailing wit and easy grace. Boileau called him "the great observer." For Molière knew how to penetrate to the very roots of human absurdity. Despite the complexity of some of his plots, his plays are comedies of character rather than of situation. The large gallery of portraits he has left us is a tribute both to his genius and his humanity. His portraiture of human foibles, his understanding of the human character are everywhere true to the facts of life.

There is one trait which distinguishes him from nearly all writers of comedy: the fact that he is consistently a moralist. He rarely wrote a play that was not concerned with the improvement of manners. He castigated hypocrisy, pretentiousness, dishonesty, excess, folly, perverted values, injustice in family-relationships wherever he found them. He is so great an artist that he never seems to be in the pulpit, but at the core of every one of his major works is great moral earnestness. Although some of his critics objected to the almost colloquial ease of his lines, there is no writer of the period who has more natural elegance or who more insistently advocates the classic love of moderation in all things. His plots are constructed with admirable fluency; incident follows incident with an air of naturalness. Nothing is strained, nothing seems improbable. Most remarkable of all, even his most farcical stories are elevated by his intelligence to the plane of high comedy.

SELECTED BIBLIOGRAPHY

TRANSLATIONS

———, *Plays: The High-Brow Ladies, The School for Wives, Tartuffe, The Misanthrope, The Physician in Spite of Himself* (The Modern Library, 1924).

Baker, H. & Miller, J., *Comedies* (Everyman's Library, E. P. Dutton & Co., 1929).

Bishop, M., *The Would-Be-Invalid* (Crofts Classics, Appleton-Century-Crofts, 1950).

Frank W. (ed.), *Plays by Molière* (Boni & Liveright, 1924).

Grebanier, B., *The Misanthrope* (Barron's Educational Series, 1959).

Gregory, Lady, *The Kiltartan Molière* (Maunsel & Co., 1910).

Morley, H. (ed.), *Plays from Molière by English Dramatists* (G. Routledge & Sons, 1885).

Van Laun, H., *The Dramatic Works of Molière* (W. Paterson, 1875-76).

Waldinger, R., *The Learned Ladies* (Barron's Educational Series, 1957).

    Tartuffe (Barron's Educational Series, 1959).

Wall, C. H., *The Dramatic Works of Molière* (G. Bell & Sons, 1876-77).

Waller, A. R., *The Plays of Molière* (John Grant, 1907).

Wood, J., *Five Plays: The Would-Be-Gentleman, That Scoundrel Scapin, The Miser, Love's the Best Doctor, Don Juan* (Penguin Books, 1953).

    The Misanthrope and Other Plays: The Misanthrope, The Sicilian, Tartuffe, A Doctor in Spite of Himself, The Imaginary Invalid (Penguin Books, 1959).

STUDIES

Ashton, H., *Molière* (G. Routledge & Sons, 1930).

Auerbach, F. (tr. by W. Trask), "The *Faux Dévot*" in *Mimesis* (Princeton, 1953).

Bagley, C. R., *An Introduction to French Literature of the Seventeenth Century* (D. Appleton-Century, 1937).

Bungener, F., *The Preacher and the King* (Gould & Lincoln, 1854).

Cairncross, J., *New Light on Molière* (Priv. Pr., Geneva, 1956).

Cauldwell, H., *Introduction to French Classicism* (The Macmillan Co., 1931).

Chapman, P. A., *The Spirit of Molière* (Princeton University Press, 1940).

Chatfield-Taylor, H. C., *Molière* (Duffield & Co., 1906).

Crump, P. E., *Nature in the Age of Louis XIV* (G. Routledge & Sons, 1928).

Hall, H. G., *Tartuffe* (Barron's Studies in French Literature, 1960).

Mantzius, K., *A History of Theatrical Art, Vol. IV* (Duckworth & Co., 1905).

Matthews, B., *Molière, His Life and Works* (C. Scribner's Sons, 1926).

Moore, W. G., "*Tartuffe* and the Comic Principle," in *Modern Language Review*, January, 1948.

Perry, H. T. E., *Masters of Dramatic Comedy* (Harvard University Press, 1939).

Pierce, W. T., *The Bourgeois from Molière to Beaumarchais* (Johns Hopkins Press, 1907).

Sainte-Beuve, C. A. (K. Wermeley, tr.), *Portraits of the Seventeenth Century* (G. P. Putnam's Sons, 1904).

Stewart, H. F. & Tilley, A. A., *The Classical Movement in French Literature* (Cambridge University Press, 1923).

Tilley, A. A., *From Montaigne to Molière* (Cambridge University Press, 1923).

    Molière (Cambridge University Press, 1921).

Trollope, H. M., *The Life of Molière* (E. P. Dutton & Co., 1905).

Turnell, M., *The Classical Moment* (H. Hamilton, 1947).

Stoll, E. E., *Shakespeare and Other Masters* (Harvard University Press, 1940).

Vincent, L. H., *Molière* (Houghton, Mifflin & Co., 1902).

Wheatley, K. E., *Molière and Terence* (University of Texas Press, 1931).

Wilcox, J., *The Relation of Molière to Restoration Comedy* (Columbia University Press, 1938).

Wright, C. H. C., *French Classicism* (Harvard University Press, 1920).

NOTES

NOTES

NOTES

NOTES

NOTES

NOTES

NOTES

NOTES

NOTES

NOTES

NOTES

NOTES

NOTES

NOTES

NOTES

NOTES

NOTES

NOTES